CONTENTS

HOUSEPLANT BASICS   4

CHOOSING HOUSEPLANTS..5
MOVING HOUSEPLANTS 6
CONTAINERS 7
GROWING MEDIA 8
REPOTTING AND POTTING UP 10
LIGHT...11
WATERING...12
TEMPERATURE 13
HUMIDITY..14
FEEDING 14
SUMMERING PLANTS..15
VACATIONS...15
PREVENTING PROBLEMS 15
CLEANING 16
PRUNING AND STAKING..16
PROPAGATION...18
HOUSEPLANT FIRST AID 23

HOUSEPLANT SELECTION   24

Seven charts to help you select the houseplants
that best fit your home's conditions, your
decorating needs, and your gardening skills.

HOUSEPLANTS A TO Z   26

Photographs and brief but thorough care
instructions for more than 190 popular foliage,
blooming, and succulent houseplants.

INDEX   125

Four pages of cross-referenced index entries to
help you find the plant you want, whether you
know it by its botanical or common name.

Houseplant
BASICS

WITH PROPER CARE, HOUSEPLANTS CAN BRING IN-
DOORS THE LUSH GREENS OF TROPICAL FOLIAGE
AND THE COLORS AND SWEET SCENTS OF BLOOM.
LOOK TO THIS CHAPTER FOR GENERAL ADVICE.
THEN TURN TO PAGE 26 FOR SPECIFICS.

Choosing Houseplants

Each of the more than 190 houseplant types and varieties detailed later in this book is unique in color and form, and each has special light and temperature requirements. Select plants that match your decorating needs and the growing conditions in your home. Seeing the plants and reading about their peculiarities in "Houseplants A to Z," pages 26–124, will help you a lot with this process. Charts on pages 24–25 also are designed to help you select and place plants properly.

Foliage plants are the backbone of most houseplant collections. In full form year-round, they provide varied shades of green, a rich variety of textures, and shapes from massive to minute. Plants can be found to match the conditions in most any spot, from a bright corner by a window to a dim nook in a bathroom. How you choose to display the plants is up to you, but all can be made to match interior design and decor tastefully.

Flowering plants add bright splashes of color and exquisite scents. Some are difficult to raise indoors and are seasonal gift plants. Others are not quite so temperamental and will bloom year after year. The secret is to match your and your plants' needs so that you both get what you want: healthy plants that provide stunning color and delicate scent for as long as possible.

WHERE TO BUY

Most of the plants listed in "Houseplants A to Z" are commonly available in florist shops and garden centers. Buy from reputable stores where you know plants receive proper care. If the plants in a store look healthy, you can feel reasonably confident that the plants you buy there will be vigorous and long-lived.

You may have to order some of the more unusual plants discussed in this book through catalogs. Plant societies often are an overlooked source of unusual plants or unusual varieties of more common plants. Most garden magazines also have sections with sources for rare or exotic plants.

Buy from companies that offer money-back guarantees. If you receive damaged, dry, or diseased plants from a mail-order company, return them at once for a full refund. Ordering plants through the mail always is risky since plants can be damaged in transit by temperatures too high or too low. Most companies, however, stand behind their plants and replace them if necessary.

Many indoor gardeners start rare and unusual plants from seeds ordered through mail-order companies. Starting plants from seed is one of the most rewarding aspects of indoor gardening, one that

saves you lots of money while giving tremendous satisfaction. Companies often send detailed growing instructions with the seeds. If you can't find a seed in a catalog, try one of the seed exchanges now included in many garden magazines as a service to readers. You might try starting plants, too, from cuttings taken off friends' plants.

Checking Plants at Store

Check plants carefully before buying them. Look for insects on the stem and undersides of leaves, and at leaf axils (where the branches join the stem). Do not buy wilted, yellowed, or discolored plants.

WHAT TO LOOK FOR

Examine plants carefully before buying (see photo, above). Foliage plants should be lush and full, and have good color. Stems and leaves should be firm, not wilted or distorted, and roughly equal on all sides. New growth should be evident. The foliage should be natural, not covered with a thin film of polish or wax.

When choosing a flowering plant, don't pick one with flowers in full bloom. Though dramatic, the blossoms on plants in full flower often fade quickly. Plants with numerous buds, but fewer blooms, generally last much longer. As with all general rules, there are exceptions. Buy anthurium in full bloom since its flowers last for several months.

Check each plant for disease and insects. Look closely where the branches join the stem. Avoid any plant already infected with mealybug, red spider mite, or scale. These pests will quickly infect the rest of your plants.

Insects are especially common on plants imported from areas where they are grown outdoors. Also, plants displayed outdoors during warmer months may attract insects.

Check the soil. Feel it with your fingers. It shouldn't be too loose or too compacted. Some growers save money by using ordinary garden soil for potting. This soil usually turns hard as brick when dry, a condition that stunts plant growth. Repot plants with poor soil if necessary.

Houseplant BASICS

MOVING HOUSEPLANTS

Once you've selected and paid for your plants, make sure they're packaged properly before taking them home. Poorly packaged plants tip over or bounce around, which can damage branches. Good growers will package plants for you or give you appropriate containers so your plants can reach your home undamaged.

Cold and heat can harm houseplants, too. During the winter, warm up your car and wrap your plants before taking them outside. Never leave your plants in a cold car while you do additional shopping. During the summer, buy plants with well-moistened soil, because dry plants do not resist heat well. Have overly dry plants watered. Let the water drain, then pack the plants.

If left unprotected, houseplants can be damaged by wind. If you must transport a large plant in the open, cover its leafy branches to prevent them from drying out. Wrap heavy plastic or cloth around the branches and tie it to the stem. Remove the wrap as soon as you arrive home.

If your concern is not getting plants home from the store, but moving your plants from one home to another, be aware that moving companies rarely handle plants properly. You may have to question several companies about their methods of transporting plants to find one that really knows this delicate phase of the business.

LABELING

As soon as you arrive home with a plant, check for a label. If one came with the plant, note on the back with permanent marker the date of purchase and source of the plant. If no label was included, make your own, noting plant type and variety, too.

It's surprising how easy it is to forget all of this information after a few months. Knowing exactly what plant and variety you're growing is important when it comes to determining cultural needs and solving problems. It's also fun to be able to identify your winners and know how long you've owned a plant. With proper labeling, you can keep track of good and bad plant sources and more easily obtain refunds when appropriate.

Containers

Most houseplants today are sold in standard plastic pots. Some plant owners prefer to replace these pots. They choose from pots that come in an almost-infinite variety of materials, types, sizes, and colors. When choosing a container, consider your plant's needs, your decorating needs, and your houseplant skills.

At its simplest level, the purpose of a container is to hold the right amount of growing medium for the plant. In other words, the container you choose should match the size of your plant. Small plants should be in small containers and large plants in large containers.

Plants that are too small for their containers look out of proportion and grow poorly since the soil stays overly moist for too long a time. Plants that are too large for their containers also look out of proportion. They become root-bound (roots fill up the whole pot, causing stunted growth), and often topple over, since their pots don't have enough weight to hold them up.

The best pots have holes in their bottoms for excess water to drain out. If water collects in the bottom of a pot, it can cause root rot, which eventually kills plants.

Because of these holes, each pot needs a plastic or clay saucer underneath it to prevent excess water from spilling onto your carpet, floor, or furniture. Many hanging pots have built-in saucers to collect excess water. Be careful when watering plants in these pots since their saucers are shallow and water sometimes overflows.

A few of the most decorative pots have no drainage holes. Knowing how much to water plants in these pots is difficult and requires far more skill than watering plants in traditional pots does. Still, many indoor gardeners use these lovely pots with great success by carefully avoiding overwatering.

The beginning houseplant grower can get the look of these ornamental pots without the risk of root rot simply by putting the less attractive pots (with their saucers) inside bigger, prettier pots, such as jardinieres or wicker baskets. This way, water drains well, but you keep the desired look.

At one time, the clay pot was the most common container for indoor plants. Clay pots are attractive, heavy (ideal for big plants), and porous (excellent for bromeliads, cacti, ferns, orchids, and succulents). Unfortunately, clay pots break easily, need to be watered frequently, and are hard to clean. They also are becoming expensive.

The most popular container today is the plastic pot. It comes in an assortment of colors and is lightweight (plastic is an excellent material for hanging baskets), easy to clean, and inexpensive. One major advantage of plastic over clay is that, because plastic does not absorb moisture from the soil the way clay does, plants in plastic pots don't need to be watered as frequently. Normally, plastic is quite tough, but it can break in cold weather.

Other materials for houseplant containers include metal, basketry, treated or rot-resistant wood, glazed pottery, and glass. Containers made from these materials, though, usually are used only as bigger pots to surround smaller, more-functional ones, or for other special purposes.

Pots come in a variety of sizes. The width of the opening at the top determines the size. A 4-inch pot has an opening 4 inches wide. Most pots are as deep as they are wide. Azalea pots, however, are only three-fourths as deep as they are wide; bulb pots are half as deep. Growers have found that some plants look and grow better in shallow pots.

CLEANING POTS
Keep pots clean to prevent disease (see photo, below). If you plan to reuse a pot, clean it well both inside and out. Clay pots often get a white crust on them after prolonged use. To remove this crust, scrub with a steel wool pad or stiff brush in a vinegar and water solution. If the crust is thick, brush first with a dry steel wool pad. Rinse pots, then soak them in a bleach solution (1 part bleach to 9 parts water) for 30 minutes. Rinse again.

CLEANING CLAY POTS

To avoid infecting plants with disease, scrub all used pots carefully, inside and out, before reusing. To remove salt and clinging earth from clay pots, rub with steel wool and diluted vinegar. Then soak pots in a bleach solution.

GROWING PLANTS IN WATER

For best results, use opaque jars when growing plants in water. To keep the water fresh, change it frequently and add small bits of charcoal. Add water-soluble fertilizers for rich foliage.

Clean plastic pots with a cloth dipped in warm, soapy water. Scrub the pot until it's completely free of soil and grime. Soak the pot in a bleach solution as you would a clay pot.

Sterilizing pots is especially important if you intend to start seeds in them. Nonsterile pots often contain bacteria that can infect the soil, causing seedlings to topple over from a condition called *damping-off*. The condition is serious because it can kill all seedlings if not prevented in the first place or treated with fungicide when first noticed.

GROWING MEDIA

Soil or one of its substitutes is the almost-universal growing medium. Plants in stores are sold potted in soil. Water, however, works well for many plants (see photo, above), and can replace soil for growing plants at home.

WATER
When growing plants in water, avoid the use of softened water, which contains salts. Rainwater is excellent in some areas, but air pollution makes it less ideal in others. Both well water and bottled water are good media for plants.

Change water frequently to keep it aerated and fresh. Add charcoal to the water to keep it fresh longer. You'll find bags filled with small pieces of charcoal in many florist shops.

To encourage better root growth, choose opaque containers. Fertilize with liquid fish emulsion or other water-soluble material as you would plants grown in soil.

A few of the plants that thrive in water are arrowhead vine, coleus, Chinese evergreen, croton, devil's ivy, dieffenbachia, dracaena, English ivy, grape ivy, philodendron, Swedish ivy, sweet potato, and wandering Jew.

SOIL AND SOIL SUBSTITUTES

The ideal potting soil is solid enough to anchor roots, but loose enough to allow quick root growth, good drainage, and the free flow of air. It also retains moisture without getting soggy. Ordinary garden soil is solid, but it often compacts into a hard ball. Avoid its use for houseplants.

The traditional houseplant potting soil contains equal parts black loam (good garden soil), peat moss, and perlite. The garden soil is quite heavy and provides a solid base of earth for the plant. Its finer particles (mainly clay) retain nutrients. Peat moss is light and absorbs lots of water, keeping the growing medium moist. The perlite acts as a spacer so that roots can grow freely. It also keeps the soil from compacting and becoming waterlogged. A tip: Dry peat moss sheds cool water. When moistening peat for the first time, use hot water.

Many other materials can replace these three (see photo, right, top). Coarse sand and vermiculite are two of the most common. Shredded bark and charcoal are used in special instances, as for growing orchids and bromeliads. To replace peat moss, some gardeners use compost, leaf mold (decomposed leaves), or rotted horse manure.

Buy or make your own soil mix (see photos, right, bottom). Either way, be sure the mix has been sterilized to kill disease and weed seeds. Most (not all) commercial soil mixes are sterile. Read packages carefully; if a soil mix is sterile, the package will say so. You can sterilize your own mix at home by baking pans of soil and other ingredients in an oven, but be prepared for a messy, smelly, and time-consuming job. If you're not up to the task, take the gamble and use your own, unsterilized mix for mature plants, but buy sterile growing medium to start seedlings.

Note that *potting soil* is a generic term, virtually meaningless in the marketplace. Tests indicate a wide range of materials used in making potting soils, little uniformity, varied chemical analyses, varied fertility, and varied amounts of viable weed seed. Cost also is no indication of quality. Compare and settle on a brand through experience.

The pH (relative acidity or alkalinity) of soils is rarely a problem for most indoor plants. Repeated watering with hard water does cause soil to turn alkaline. If your water is hard, replace soil annually. Note that some plants—particularly azalea (rhododendron) and camellia—must have acid soil to grow properly. The simplest way to treat soils for these plants is to use an acid fertilizer (available at florist shops). Alternatives are to add acidic peat moss (sold in garden centers) to the soil or to saturate the soil with a vinegar solution (1 tablespoon per gallon of water).

CHOOSING A SOIL MIXTURE

Buy potting soils of various makeups premixed, or mix your own, using the ingredients that work best for you. Clockwise from right, below: vermiculite, sand, black loam, perlite, peat moss.

MIXING POTTING SOIL

1 Sterilize garden earth before mixing in other ingredients. Place in pan, seal with foil, and bake in a 200° oven until a meat thermometer registers 150° to 180° for 30 minutes. If other ingredients aren't sterile, mix with earth and bake.

2 Once ingredients are sterile and cool, thoroughly mix equal parts garden soil, perlite, and peat moss. This mixture yields an all-purpose potting soil. Vary ingredients and proportions for special plants, like cactus and orchid.

POTTING UP A PLANT

1 When potting up, choose a pot one size larger than the pot the plant is in now. Make sure the pot is clean. Place a shard from a broken pot or a piece of screen over the drainage hole to keep soil from washing out.

2 Wet the soil the day before removing a plant. To remove, hold your hand against the soil and around the stem, turn the pot upside down, and tap the rim on a surface. Once it's loose, grasp the plant near the soil; pull gently.

3 Keep the root ball as intact as possible, unless the roots have become a snarl. If the roots are tangled, lightly loosen the outer part of the root ball with your hands or a knife, being careful not to damage the delicate roots.

4 Place some soil in the new pot, then position the plant on top. Adjust plant to leave enough space below the rim for easy watering. Fill with soil around the root ball, burying plant to same level. Tap pot; add soil as needed. Water.

REPOTTING AND POTTING UP

Because plants at garden centers and nurseries often are root-bound, and because the soil mixes the plants come in sometimes are not ideal, you'll often need to repot or pot up new plants immediately after purchase. Many plants also require regular potting up throughout their lifetimes.

Taking a plant out of a pot and putting it back in the same or same-size pot is called *repotting*. Taking a plant out of a pot and putting it into a larger pot is called *potting up* or *potting on*.

Plants regularly need potting up to keep their roots from compacting, a condition that harms most houseplants (although a few tolerate it well). Signs of compacted root growth include slow growth, quick wilting after flowering, yellow lower leaves, small new leaves, and roots growing through the drain hole.

Check the roots of fast-growing plants frequently to see if they are compacted. Slow-growing plants usually need potting up no more than once a year, or even less often. Plants that like being root-bound are noted in "Houseplants A to Z," pages 26–124.

For plants that go dormant, repot or pot up (if root-bound) at the end of the dormant period, just before the plant's active growing season.

The day before repotting or potting up, moisten the soil. This makes it easier to get the plant out and shields the plant from some of the trauma caused by the process. Soil should be uniformly moist, not dry or soggy.

When potting up, generally go up one pot size only (see photo 1, left). If a plant is in a 4-inch pot, go up to a 5-inch (not a 6-inch) pot. Put a crockery shard or piece of screen over the new pot's hole.

To remove a plant from a pot, turn it upside down while supporting it with one hand (see photo 2). Tap the pot gently. If the plant won't slide out, run a knife along the inside of the pot. Flip it over and tap again. Occasionally, you may have to tug gently on the stem. To remove spiny plants, grip them with folded newspaper. To remove larger plants, seek the help of a friend.

Keep the root ball as intact as possible, unless it's snarled. If that's happened, loosen some roots around the edges and bottom (see photo 3).

Bury the root ball at the same depth it was before (see photo 4). Leave enough space below the rim—¼ inch to 1 inch depending on the size of the pot—for easy watering. Press added soil firmly around the plant. Tap the pot to even the soil and eliminate air pockets. Add more soil. Water plant immediately. Keep plant in indirect light until it shows new growth. Keep soil moist, never soggy.

LIGHT

Light is vital to plants, yet each type of plant, and sometimes individual plants within a type, demand different amounts of it. Each home, too, presents entirely different conditions. That's why you should plan on experimenting with each plant until you find the spot that yields best performance.

There are some general rules, but these all have exceptions. For the most part, flowering plants need more light than foliage plants. Yet croton, a foliage plant, needs lots of light to keep its vibrant leaf color. Most plants with thick, fleshy leaves need little light, yet cacti and succulents thrive in bright light.

Some plants flower according to how long light is present each day, rather than how intense it is. Christmas cactus, chrysanthemum, kalanchoe, and poinsettia are examples of plants that need short days (long nights) to flower properly.

The specific needs of many common plants are outlined in "Houseplants A to Z," pages 26–124. Also see page 24 for a chart that helps you find the plants that fit your home's light conditions.

Fortunately, if other conditions—water, soil, and humidity—are right, many plants can live under less-than-perfect light.

NATURAL LIGHT

To detemine the intensity of the light on a given spot in your home, place an object there and check the shadow. The more intense the light, the more defined the shadow. Generally, a south exposure is the brightest. East and west windows can be bright, but usually not as bright as south windows. North windows generally are the dimmest.

Light varies considerably by time of year. Light also varies by what's nearby. It can reflect off light-colored buildings or snow, or be blocked by trees, shades, and awnings.

Light intensity drops dramatically as you move from the source. Plants near a window receive far more light than ones several feet away, even though the room may seem flooded with light.

To understand the terms used in "Houseplants A to Z," follow this guide. *High light* is found in a greenhouse or by a window with a southern or southwestern exposure. This is intense light, as strong as can be found indoors. It also is called *full sun. Medium light* refers to direct exposure from an east or west window. Also receiving medium (or what's often called *bright indirect*) light are spots near a filtered southern or southwestern exposure (or some distance from a similar exposure that's unfiltered). *Low light* is found near north windows. The light several feet from an east or west

window or far from a southern or southwestern exposure (in both cases, often called *indirect light*) also qualifies as low light. Low light is common in corners and bathrooms. It is not total darkness.

Your plants will let you know when the light is not right (see photos, below). Insufficient light causes spindly stems, yellow foliage, and leaf drop. Too much light causes leaf burn or pale foliage.

ARTIFICIAL LIGHT

Many houseplants thrive in artificial light. The most effective and inexpensive light source for houseplants is a fluorescent tube.

Carefully position plants under the light source (as close as 6 inches, never more than 15 inches away). Keep lights on for as many as 16 hours a day depending on the plant.

Again, your plants will tell you how much light they need. Flowering plants fail to bud or bloom in poor artificial light. Foliage plants needing more light get tall and spindly. Foliage plants exposed to too much light often look ghostly or faded.

TOO MUCH, TOO LITTLE LIGHT

This peperomia's sun-bleached leaves—sickly, lifeless, and colorless—show the effects of too much intense sun. Remove the lackluster leaves (they won't turn green again) and move the plant away from direct sun.

When mature leaves turn yellow and new leaves grow small and spindly, as on this schefflera, the culprit is too little light, or a lack of fertilizer or water. If the plant is in a room with low light, move it to where it will get more sun.

Houseplant
BASICS

WATERING TECHNIQUES

For most plants, test soil moisture by dipping your finger an inch or more into the soil. If dry, add water. If moist, recheck later. Wet-loving plants may need water once the soil surface dries. For desert plants, let most of the soil dry.

Use a long-spout watering can to reach all sides of a pot easily and avoid spills. If you have many plants, buy a large watering can. Saturate the soil around each plant with tepid water.

Pour until water runs out the drainage hole. Let the plant drain, then dump the excess water from the saucer. Water left to stand more than a day or two can cause roots to rot.

If you've forgotten to water a plant and its soil has pulled away from the sides of the pot, push the soil back in place before watering. Otherwise, water will pour straight down the gap to the saucer under the pot.

To increase the light intensity, use more powerful lights, use more tubes, place the tubes closer together, use white reflectors, move plants closer to tubes, or burn lights longer. Match the length of exposure to the needs of the plant as outlined in "Houseplants A to Z."

When growing plants under fluorescent tubes, rotate them regularly since the light at the end of the tubes often is weaker than that in the middle. Experiment with lights from different makers and a combination of fluorescent and incandescent bulbs for a broader color spectrum. Be wary of heat generated by incandescent bulbs; it can burn plants if they are placed too close.

WATERING

The first rule of watering is that there is no set rule. Each plant has different needs (see "Houseplants A to Z," pages 26–124, for the specific watering needs of many common plants). Pot size and home humidity can affect watering frequency, too.

Generally, try as best you can to give plants what they would get in their natural environments. Some plants need a period of dry soil for days or weeks. Others need more regular watering, with the soil allowed to dry between each drink. Still others prefer consistently moist soil. Many plants go through phases of growth when they require more or less water.

Match watering frequency to the plant's needs and growth patterns. Watch for wilting—a sign of water stress. Also watch for leaf drop or yellowing.

Do not kill your plants with kindness. More plants die from overwatering than any other cause (see photos, opposite). When you overwater, the soil gets so soggy that oxygen cannot reach the roots. Soggy soil also encourages the growth of certain bacteria, which can eventually cause root rot, an often-fatal condition.

Test soil regularly by sticking a finger an inch or more into it (see photo 1, left). Use a spoon or similar object if you don't want a dirty finger.

Buy a good watering can (see photo 2), one with a long spout and a large opening at the end of the spout. If you have a lot of plants, buy a large can.

Rainwater, well water, and bottled water generally agree best with plants. Collect rainwater in a barrel or plastic garbage can at the base of a downspout. Keep in mind, though, that in some parts of the country, the air sometimes pollutes rainwater. Similarly, well water sometimes can be too alkaline for acid-loving plants. Bottled water is excellent, but expensive. Chlorinated water will not damage houseplants.

EFFECTS OF TOO MUCH WATER

This creeping charlie shows signs of severe overwatering: soft stems, drooping and paling leaves. Its root ball (right) is soggy. To revive an overwatered plant, first withhold water. If that doesn't work, repot once soggy soil has dried a little.

Tap water is OK if not too hard, but avoid softened water. Softened water contains salt, which builds up in soil over a period of months. If you do use softened water, replace the soil yearly, scrubbing all deposits from the pots (see page 8).

Avoid spotting the leaves of fuzzy-leaved plants by using tepid water. Fill your watering can after each watering session and let it sit until next time. That way, the water will reach the right temperature for watering these temperamental plants.

Whenever you water plants, saturate the soil. Be bold. Water the pot until excess water drains from the bottom and collects in the dish below. If the water gets too deep in the dish, dump it to prevent root rot (see photo 3, opposite).

Pour water evenly around the plant to moisten the entire surface. If the soil has gotten too dry and pulled away from the side of the pot, push the soil back against the side before watering (see photo 4, opposite). If you don't, the water will rush down the gap and out the bottom of the pot. Then, after watering such overly dry plants once and dumping the excess water from the saucer, water again.

Water in the morning if possible. This gives any moistened foliage a chance to dry out during the day. Plants with dry foliage have less chance of contracting disease in the cool evening hours.

Water less during a plant's dormant period. Most plants grow rapidly in spring and summer and require lots of water at this time. During late fall and winter, however, they stop growing and require far less water. The opposite is true for a few plants, which may need little watering in spring and summer, and quite a bit of water during their active period in fall and winter.

TEMPERATURE

Just as plants vary in their moisture needs, so, too, do they vary in their temperature requirements. Some plants like it cool; others like it tropical (see "Houseplants A to Z," pages 26–124).

Most houseplants do well in average house temperatures. To encourage best growth, turn your thermostat down at night. Plants like a 10-degree temperature drop after dark. This drop duplicates what they experience in nature.

To grow plants that like cool conditions, keep your thermostat between 60 and 70 degrees in the day, lower at night. Many plants that go dormant in winter prefer cooler temperatures. For plants that like high temperatures, set your thermostat in the 80s during the day and lower at night.

Houseplant
BASICS

Maintaining the desired temperature is especially important to flowering plants. Azalea and Christmas cactus need temperatures near 30 degrees to form buds. Other tropical bloomers need high temperatures to flower freely.

No houseplant wants to freeze or bake. Prevent cold drafts near plants. Keep plants away from cold windows in winter. Don't let houseplants summered outside freeze in a late-spring or early-fall cold snap. Keep plants away from radiators and hot blasts of any sort.

HUMIDITY

Homes with central heating are dry during fall and winter. The same is true in summer in houses where the air conditioner runs a lot. Cacti and succulents thrive in dry conditions, but most plants don't. Either you grow plants that like or tolerate dryness (see "Houseplants A to Z," pages 26–124), or you raise the humidity in your home.

A humidifier is the simplest and most obvious solution. The added moisture benefits most houseplants. And it benefits furniture and people, too. If you don't want to buy a whole-house or room humidifier, try setting a small vaporizer near plants.

To increase humidity around an individual plant, place pebbles in the saucer below the pot. Wet the pebbles, making sure that the water does not touch the bottom of the pot.

Grouping plants helps, too, because moisture released by one plant can be picked up by another. You also can place several plants on a large tray or pan filled with pebbles and water (see photo, below left, top). Keep in mind, though, that despite their love for humidity, plants need good air circulation to ward off disease. Leaves of individual plants should not touch. This isn't always possible, but you should try to give each plant breathing room.

A technique called *double potting* (see photo, below left, bottom) is another way to bring more humidity to plants. Place a potted plant inside a larger container. Fill the space between the pots with sphagnum moss. Keep the moss saturated with water.

Finally, spray your plants frequently with a fine mist of tepid water. Mist both the tops and bottoms of leaves. Mist in the morning so that plants have a chance to dry during the day. Misting at night encourages disease. Besides increasing the humidity around plants, misting also helps deter some insects, especially red spider mites.

INCREASING THE HUMIDITY

Place an individual plant or a group of plants on a tray of wet pebbles to raise the humidity around them. Fill the tray with water until the water's surface is just below the pot bottoms. Don't overwater; the plants' roots may rot.

You can raise humidity, too, by placing a potted plant inside a larger pot. Fill the gap between the pots with sphagnum moss. Pour water over the moss until it's moist. This technique is called double potting.

FEEDING

All plants need certain chemicals to grow well. Outdoors, they send out miles of roots when they can't find what they need nearby. Indoors, though, they don't have that option. So provide your houseplants with regular feedings of organic (natural) or inorganic (man-made) fertilizers.

The three major nutrients that plants receive from fertilizers are nitrogen, phosphorus, and potassium (usually abbreviated as N, P, and K on packages). Nitrogen is important for good foliage, phosphorus helps roots grow, and potassium is vital for good blooming.

The percentages of the major nutrients contained in any given fertilizer are listed on the label. A 10-10-10 fertilizer is made up of 10 percent nitrogen, 10 percent phosphorus, and 10 percent potassium; the other 70 percent is either organic or inert material. The percentages of the individual chemicals vary considerably by the product, but they always are listed in the same order. The higher the number, the more chemical present.

Common organic fertilizers are blood meal, bonemeal, cow manure, fish emulsion, and kelp products. Chemical fertilizers are sold under a variety of product names. The chemical analysis varies by brand. Read labels carefully.

Some of these fertilizers are formulated with specific plants in mind. A few plants—such as azalea (rhododendron), camellia, and gardenia—need acid fertilizers, which keep the pH of the soil low. Other plants need varying amounts of specific chemicals, and the formulas for these plants reflect this.

You can apply fertilizers in a number of ways. Mix them in a dry form into the soil either as a powder or in tiny time-release capsules. Or dilute them in water and pour them onto the soil at intervals. Or spray some forms (especially kelp) directly onto the leaves. The choice is up to you.

Organic fertilizers work slowly. It takes time for them to break down in the soil and release nutrients. Some time-release chemical formulas also break down slowly, releasing nutrients over a long period of time. Most chemical fertilizers, however, work rapidly, giving plants a quick boost.

Before applying any fertilizer, thoroughly moisten the soil. Never use more than the recommended dose; too much fertilizer can burn roots and kill plants. In fact, it's generally better to use less than the recommended amount and apply the fertilizer more frequently. This is especially true for chemical fertilizers, which tend to be more caustic than organic ones.

The goal of fertilizing is to encourage regular—not rampant—growth during a plant's main growing season. Do not feed plants when they're dormant, usually in fall and winter, although some plants go dormant in spring and summer.

Certain plants require special feedings. In "Houseplants A to Z," pages 26–124, we note the specific needs of individual plants.

SUMMERING PLANTS

Most indoor plants like to be moved outdoors for the summer. Do this after all danger of frost has passed. Move plants first into shade, then into indirect light, and finally, if they are full-sun plants, into bright light. This gradual process, known as *hardening off*, takes about 14 days. Plants moved too quickly into outdoor brightness may fade, drop leaves, or show stunted growth.

Place houseplants outside in locations that match their indoor light preferences: sun-loving plants in full-sun positions, shade-loving plants under trees for filtered light. Water plants frequently. Gently mist their foliage to increase humidity, kill insects, and cleanse. At season's end, spray plants with insecticide before bringing them indoors. Do not let the plants suffer frost damage. Better to bring them in too early than too late.

GOING ON VACATION

Keep plants healthy for up to three weeks while you're away by watering them, then covering them with makeshift plastic tents. Use bamboo stakes or bent wire clothes hangers to support the plastic above the plant's leaves.

VACATIONS

If you're going to be away from your plants for a long weekend, soak them thoroughly a day before leaving. Drain excess water from saucers below pots. Group plants on pebble trays or double-pot plants (see photos, opposite). Remove dead leaves and flower buds. In winter, lower the thermostat.

For longer stays away, if you can't find a dependable plant sitter, cover each plant or small group of plants with plastic (see photo, above). Use bamboo stakes or metal hangers to keep the plastic above the leaves. Place plants out of direct light. Turn thermostat down. Such flimsy terrariums will keep plants alive up to 3 weeks.

Another idea: Lay plastic in your bathtub. Cover the plastic with newspaper, then wet the papers. Thoroughly water your plants, then set them in the tub. Cover with plastic to keep humidity high.

PREVENTING PROBLEMS

Diseases and pests can threaten the health of your plants (see chart, page 23, for remedies). Fortunately, you can take steps to prevent problems.

First, isolate new plants for several weeks until you're sure they're healthy and pest free. Return diseased or pest-ridden plants immediately. Wash your hands thoroughly after touching an infected plant. Discard old plants that are beyond saving.

Clean pots before using them again (see page 8). Remove all dead leaves and spent blossoms, and clean plants often (see pages 16–17). Water and mist in the morning. Follow as closely as possible the exact cultural requirements for each plant.

If insects invade a plant, first try washing them away with soapy water. If that doesn't work, use chemical sprays. Spray outside if possible.

CLEANING

Keep plants clean to prevent disease (see photos, right and opposite, left). Remove yellow or brown leaves immediately. Pull or snip faded blossoms. Pick up leaves or flowers that drop on the soil.

Spray foliage often with tepid water in a shower or sink. Use medium force. Wrap plastic around plant bases to keep soil in pots. Let plants drip-dry.

Regularly wipe dust from thick-leaved plants with damp cotton. Use a paintbrush or similar brush to clean hairy-leaved plants. Because leaves are easily damaged, always support them with one hand while you wipe or brush with the other.

Avoid leaf polishes, which can block breathing pores. If you keep leaves clean and plants healthy, good color and shine will come naturally.

PRUNING AND STAKING

Carefully prune your houseplants—especially larger treelike ones with many branches (see photos, opposite, bottom right)—to control their size and make them look more attractive and uniform. Prune when a plant is actively growing or soon after it blooms. (Plants with special pruning needs are noted in "Houseplants A to Z," pages 26–124.)

For most plants, one of the most valuable pruning techniques is to pinch off growing tips (see photo, opposite, top right). This encourages side growth, which makes a plant full and bushy. To get even more bushiness, pinch off the tips of the new side growth. Start pinching when plants are young. Pinch just above a node (where leaf stem and branch meet). Do not pinch Norfolk Island pines, all palms, or plants that grow rosettes or crowns (African violet, for example).

Another good technique is to train flowers—such as coleus, geranium, and lantana—into tree forms, often called *standards*. Start with a flower that has a strong central stem. Remove all growth but the growing tip and a few upper leaves. Tie the stem to a tall stake with wire twists, tying tightly around the stake and loosely around the stem. Avoid twine. When the plant reaches desired height, pinch the growing tip to stop upward growth. The plant then will produce numerous side branches at the stem top, creating an attractive bush that sits atop the stem like tree foliage.

Most plants do not require staking. For those that do, use unobtrusive stakes. Try single bamboo poles, trellises, wire or cane hoops, or moss sticks (chicken-wire tubes stuffed with sphagnum moss). Follow the tying guidelines given above, unless the plant climbs on its own.

CLEANING TECHNIQUES

Wash plants often in lukewarm water to rid them of dust and insects. Don't use cold water; it may spot leaves. Place small plants in a sink, large plants in a shower. Let plants drip-dry before placing them in sun.

Clean the leaves of large plants by wiping them with a moist cloth or damp cotton. Support the leaves with one hand to avoid bruising or cracking them. Do not use oils or polishes to make leaves shine; they can block pores.

Remove dust from African violets and other fuzzy-leaved plants with a soft-bristle paintbrush. Or use a soft toothbrush, pipe cleaner, or discarded fuzzy leaf. Stroke from the base of the leaf to the tip.

One simple way to clean small plants (especially those with fuzzy leaves) is to support them and their soil with your fingers, turn them upside down, and swish their leaves in tepid water. Let the plants drip-dry out of the sun.

Remove all dead or yellowing leaves regularly. Pick up any that fall on the soil. For ferns, reach under the green fronds and cut the brown leaf stalks at the soil line. Shorten or remove any leafless, stringlike stems, too.

Remove withered blossoms to keep your plants healthy and encourage further blooming. Pick up any flowers that fall on the soil to prevent disease.

PINCHING OFF GROWING TIPS

Encourage bushier growth by pinching a plant's growing tips just above where branches and leaf stems meet. For the most side growth, start when plants are young; do often.

PRUNING GANGLY TREES

1 Prune indoor trees for sturdier growth and a more pleasing shape. Prune dead or dying branches, too. The weeping fig at right is basically healthy, but it needs shaping. Several dead branches at its base need to be removed.

2 First determine the cuts that will yield the best shape. Then, with sharp pruning shears, cut the overgrown branches just above leaf buds. New growth will appear behind where branches are pruned.

STARTING SEED

1 Fill tray or pot with sterile medium, mist with water, then top with ¼ inch of milled sphagnum moss. Press moss with book. Sprinkle seeds across moss surface or into shallow rows.

2 Cover larger seeds with a sprinkling of moss. Pat smaller seeds into moss. Mist again. Cover tray with glass or plastic; place on heating pad or refrigerator. Place in light suggested on packet. Mist when moss begins to dry.

3 Remove glass when seedlings pop through moss. Move seedlings to brighter light. Transplant when second set of leaves develops. Dig seedlings up gently, holding by one of the leaves, not the stem.

4 Give each seedling its own small pot, filled to within ½ inch of top with light soil. Firm the soil around the base of each stem, making sure not to bury the leaves. Water immediately. Move plants steadily into brighter light.

PROPAGATION

You can enlarge your houseplant collection inexpensively by propagating the plants you already have using cuttings, divisions, runners, or offsets. You also can grow many houseplants from seed. Two other techniques—air layering and ground layering—help you renew plants that have grown too big or leggy.

SEEDS

Seeds are an inexpensive and satisfying way to start many houseplants, including asparagus fern, bromeliads, cacti, coleus, gloxinia, impatiens, and kalanchoe. But, because your plants won't be of display size for many months, you'll need patience.

Buy seed from a reputable company. For best germination, use fresh seed. If you have to store seed, keep it in dry containers in a cool, dark place.

Sow seeds when the seed packet directs. Plant on a small or large scale. A 6-inch pot easily accommodates from 1 to 100 seedlings, depending on the plant grown. Use trays or flats for large quantities. Begin by placing a sterile medium of your choice—potting soil, sand, vermiculite, perlite, or peat moss—into the container you've chosen.

Moisten medium, then cover with ¼ inch of milled sphagnum moss. Press the moss with a book until it's firm. Sow the seeds across the moss surface or in shallow rows (see photo 1, left). Make these rows an inch or two apart. Pat minuscule seeds into the moss; cover larger seeds to a depth three times their width. Mist the moss until its surface glistens. Label the container.

Cover the container with plastic or glass to keep humidity high (see photo 2). To provide the necessary bottom heat, place on a heating cable or heating pad, or on top of a refrigerator. Place under fluorescent lights as directed on the seed packet. Mist with tepid water whenever the medium starts to dry. Never let seedlings dry out.

When seedlings emerge, remove the cover. Watch for a condition called *damping-off,* which rots the seedling stems and causes them to collapse. If seedlings begin to topple, increase air circulation; spray immediately with a fungicide.

When plants develop a second pair of leaves, transplant them into individual pots (see photos 3 and 4). Holding each plant gently by a leaf, dig up the root system with a tongue depressor or spoon. Keep as much soil around the roots as possible. Plant each seedling so its lower leaves remain above the soil. Keep soil moist until seedlings take root. Move plants into brighter light as they start to grow. Provide mild fertilizer—half the suggested amount diluted in water—every two weeks.

You can propagate ferns by drying the tiny dots that grow on the undersides of mature leaves, then sowing the spores that are left. But the process is extremely slow, with the ferns taking as long as two years to grow to just plantlet size.

DIVISION

Many plants produce several stems with roots attached to each stem. Each of these rooted stems can be divided from the parent plant to make a new plant. You also can divide plants that grow from bulbs and tubers, as outlined below.

To divide a multistemmed plant, first remove the plant from its pot (see page 10). Early spring generally is the best time to divide plants. Press your thumbs into the middle of the plant, grab the plant with both hands, and tug it apart (see photo, right, top). If this doesn't work, remove the soil and try again. If that fails, cut the plant with a knife.

Keep a large clump of roots with each division. Immediately pot the new plants in potting soil. Keep the soil evenly moist the next few weeks to help heal the injured roots. Place plants out of direct light until they start to grow. Move them into brighter light over a period of 10 days.

Bulb plants can be divided in a couple of ways. When a parent bulb produces small bulbs off to its side, simply divide the new bulbs from the old. Plant the new bulbs as you did the parent bulb.

Some bulbs, such as achimenes, are made up of many scales that resemble pinecones. For new plants, pull off one of these scales, pot, and water.

Caladium and tuberous begonia are among the houseplants that produce fat underground growths known as *tubers*. Cut the tubers into several pieces, making sure each division has an eye. Dust wounds with fungicide. Plant immediately.

Gloxinia and cyclamen produce underground growth somewhat similar to potatoes. Cut sections containing at least one eye from these tubers, then pot. Each section will produce a new plant.

TIP CUTTINGS

The growing tips of many plants will produce vigorous new plants when cut and rooted properly (see photos, right, bottom).

Take cuttings from healthy stock. Cut 4 to 6 inches from the end of the stem or branch. Cut just below a node (the point where a leaf joins the stem). Remove the lower leaves so that the bottom 2 to 3 inches of stem are bare. Remove any flowers or buds. Dip the cut end into rooting hormone powder, then stick it into a moist, sterile rooting medium of equal parts peat moss and perlite, keeping the leaves above the soil. Substitute coarse sand or vermiculite for the perlite, if you like.

DIVIDING ROOTS

You can use division to make two or more plants from any that have multiple stems coming up from the soil surface. Pull or cut the plants apart. Each section must have a cluster of roots. Pot each section in fresh potting soil.

TIP CUTTINGS

1 To propagate new plants from most multistemmed plants, try rooting tip cuttings. First, cut 4 to 6 inches from the tip of the main stem or side branch. Cut just below a node (where leaf and stem meet).

2 Remove the lower leaves and any flowers. Dust cut ends with rooting hormone powder, then plant in moist rooting medium (half peat moss, half perlite works well); keep leaves above soil. Or, skip powder and place in water.

3 Provide indirect light and bottom heat. When cuttings resist tugs, they are taking root. Dig up gently, check root growth, and pot up. Move cuttings in water to another rooting medium as soon as roots sprout; pot up as above.

19

Houseplant
BASICS

The gangly dieffen-bachia at right is top-heavy, which is not uncommon. Dief-fenbachias and similar plants often lose lower leaves over time. When this happens, cut top off and propagate new plants as discussed below and at right.

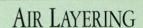

AIR LAYERING

1 Make an upward cut into the stem just below a node, at a point where you'd like new roots to grow. Cut halfway through the stem. Place toothpick or matchstick into cut to keep it open. Dust area with rooting hormone powder.

2 Place moist moss around the cut and secure it with plastic. Wrap wire twists at top and bottom. Undo top; mist moss regularly. When roots are thick, cut stem several inches below original cut; pot.

STEM CUTTINGS

Cut plant about 15 inches below bottom leaf; root in water. Pot when roots form. Cut rest of stem into short lengths, each with a node. Place horizontally in moist medium, covering node with soil. New plants will emerge.

Most tip cuttings also root easily in water, but water-grown roots are more apt to break during potting than roots started in peat and perlite. If you do root cuttings in water, use opaque containers and unsoftened water, and change the water frequently. Transplant cuttings into a peat-based rooting medium as soon as roots begin to sprout.

Keep the rooting medium constantly moist—but not soggy—to encourage quick rooting. Do not place the cuttings in direct sun. Give them indirect or artificial light. Some cuttings respond to bottom heat from a heating cable or heating pad, or the top of a refrigerator. A plastic tent around the plants sometimes helps (see page 15), but is not necessary if the soil is kept uniformly moist. Use plastic only with plants requiring high humidity.

After three to four weeks, tug gently on cuttings to see if they show resistance. If they do, pot up.

STEM AND ROOT CUTTINGS

New plants often can be produced from sections of roots or stems. Just cut roots into 2-inch sections and pot. Stem cuttings should be 4 inches long and include one or more nodes (places where leaves join the stem). Place each stem section in moist rooting medium (see photo, opposite, lower left), just covering the nodes with soil. Keep moist. In a few weeks, new growth will sprout. Pot up when roots are sufficiently strong. Dieffenbachia and dracaena often are propagated with stem cuttings.

Some cuttings work best if they include a portion of stem with a bud or leaf, forming a mallet shape. These are called *leaf-bud cuttings*. Philodendron and wax plant often are propagated this way. Plant with bud or leaf up and stem in soil.

LEAF CUTTINGS

Leaf cuttings produce new plants much the same way stem cuttings do, except a leaf stalk rather than the central stem is used. Depending on the plant, use either the whole leaf or parts of the leaf. Generally, for small-leaved plants, use the entire leaf; for large-leaved plants, leaf sections.

To propagate African violet, certain begonias, and gloxinia with a whole leaf, take at least an inch of stem with each leaf (see photo, right, top). Insert the stem into a rooting medium: water or peat-perlite mix. Keep peat-perlite mixture constantly moist. Pot up leaves in water once roots form. Pot up others once roots are established—in as little as three to four weeks, usually longer.

To propagate rex begonia with a whole leaf, set the leaf, top side up, on moist rooting medium (see photo, right, middle). Sever the veins in several places. Pin leaf so cuts are in contact with medium. Keep moist. Pot up plantlets that form at cuts.

LEAF CUTTINGS

To propagate an African violet, take at least an inch of stem with each leaf. Insert the stems into water or a peat-based mix. Pot leaves that have been in water as soon as roots form. Pot others when roots are established.

To propagate a rex begonia, set a healthy leaf, top side up, on moist growing medium. Sever a few of the veins. Pin the leaf down so the cuts come in contact with the medium. Keep moist. Pot the plantlets that grow from each cut.

To propagate a snake plant, cut a leaf into sections; indicate with angled cuts which end is bottom. Dip bottom ends in rooting powder; insert in moist rooting medium. Pot new plants that form to sides of leaf sections.

To propagate snake plant and rex begonia, sever a leaf into wedges (see photo, above, bottom). Cut begonia leaf wedges with veins. Dip bottom ends in rooting hormone powder, then insert in moist rooting medium. In a couple of months, new shoots will form at the side of each section. Pot the shoots.

AIR LAYERING

To propagate large, woody-stemmed plants, use *air layering*. This technique enables you to produce roots near any node on the stem. You then cut the stem just below the roots and pot the new plant. Air layering often is used to rejuvenate overgrown plants (see photos, opposite, center and right).

When age takes its toll on a spider plant, as it did on the one at right, it's time to root the plantlets and start over. Spider plants often become straggly. Their natural inclination is to produce new foliage and shed the old.

RUNNERS

To root plantlets that form on aerial runners, set pots filled with rooting medium nearby. Pin plantlets into medium with hairpins. Keep moist. Once plantlets root, sever stems to parent plant.

Begin by making an upward cut below a node at a point where the top section, once cut, will yield an attractive plant. Cut no more than halfway through the stem and hold the cut open with a toothpick, matchstick, or wad of sphagnum moss. Support the plant with a stake if necessary. Dust the area with rooting hormone powder. Wrap a ball of moist sphagnum moss around the cut, then enclose it in a piece of plastic wrap. Secure the wrap with string or wire twists. Some growers tape the bottom closed.

Undo the top and mist the moss regularly. In a few weeks to a few months, new roots will form in the moss ball. Once these roots are thick, open the bag and cut several inches below the root ball. Plant immediately in moist growing medium. Cut the original plant back to the soil surface; it will grow back. Or, grow additional plants by cutting the remaining stem into short sections, then potting the sections horizontally (see page 21).

Air layering usually is most successful in spring when plants are growing vigorously. Try air layering on dieffenbachia, schefflera, dracaena, and ficus family members.

GROUND LAYERING
Ground layering is similar to air layering. The difference is that the cut stem is arched over to the ground where it's anchored with a pin or weight. The cut is covered with soil. The roots then form directly into the ground.

RUNNERS
Plants that send out aerial runners and form new plantlets—spider plant, piggyback plant, flame violet, and strawberry begonia, for example—are easy to propagate (see photos, left). Just place a pot filled with peat-based rooting medium to one side. Pin the plantlet into the medium with a hairpin, then keep the medium moist until the plantlet takes root. Once rooted (the plantlet resists a gentle tug), sever the stem leading to the parent plant. Rooting usually takes about four to five weeks.

OFFSETS AND SUCKERS
To propagate plants that form offsets (offshoots) at their base—African violet, bromeliads, palms, screw pine, and succulents, for example—just cut the offsets from the parent plant and pot in standard potting mixture. Water sparingly until roots are established. Too much water causes root rot.

Suckers are similar to offsets, except that the growth to the side of the parent plant has already taken root. Cut suckers from parent plant with a sharp knife and pot in a moist growing medium. Again, avoid overwatering.

HOUSEPLANT FIRST AID

TROUBLE SIGN	CAUSE OR PEST	REMEDY
Sticky substance on leaves. Tiny, soft-bodied insects on growing tips and undersides of leaves.	Aphids	Wash leaves and stems with soapy water. Use malathion on severe infestations. Organic gardeners use sprays containing pyrethrum or rotenone, or a combination of the two.
Cottony masses where leaves join stems.	Mealybugs	Clean plants regularly with soapy water to prevent outbreaks. Dab bugs with cotton swabs saturated in rubbing alcohol. Rinse or wipe off the alcohol with warm water. Use malathion or organic sprays on severe infestations. Repeat treatment every seven to 10 days until all insects are destroyed.
Rusty, drooping leaves. Tiny webs around leaf joints.	Red spider mites	Mist plants to prevent infestations. Destroy early to prevent colonizing. Miticides, such as Kelthane (dicofol), were extremely effective, but have been taken off the market. In their place, use nicotine sulphate with extreme caution.
Sticky substance on leaves. Oval or round insects with shell-like covering on undersides of leaves or stems.	Scales	Wipe bugs off with a soapy rag. Use a toothbrush on the stems of tough plants. Rinse with clear water. Spray with malathion or organic pesticides for heavy infestations. Repeat treatment for several weeks to kill insects in different stages of growth.
Dandrufflike insects congregated on undersides of leaves or in clouds around stirred plants.	Whiteflies	Kill with malathion or organic sprays. Repeat applications because colonies have insects at different stages of growth. Insecticides are not equally effective against all growth stages. Wash hands after handling infested plants to keep from spreading invisible eggs.
Droopy plant. Slimy, soft stem base, rhizome, or tuberous root. Often a foul smell when plant is pulled from pot.	Stem rot	Prevent by not allowing water to stand in a pot's saucer for more than a day or two. Water less in winter during a plant's dormant period. Difficult to remedy: remove plant from container, cut off decayed area, repot, and water properly.
Toppled seedlings. Mushy spots at plant bases.	Damping-off	Prevent by using sterile medium to start seedlings. If damping-off occurs, water less and lower humidity. Use fungicides in severe cases.
Stunted growth. Mottled, streaked, or spotted foliage. Sunken areas on the stems.	Viruses	Destroy these plants because no cure exists. If not disposed of, they will spread disease to other plants. Do not propagate in any way since viruses can be transferred to new plants.
Buds shrivel and turn dry. Flowers drop off prematurely or do not form properly.	Uneven watering, low humidity, incorrect temperature, drafts, or shock from moves	Water more consistently. Raise humidity by misting foliage (not flowers), by double-potting, or by putting plant on a tray filled with pebbles and water. Keep temperature where it belongs for that plant. Avoid cold drafts. Do not move certain plants, such as Christmas cactus, after buds form.

HOUSEPLANTS FOR DIFFERENT LIGHT CONDITIONS

HIGH LIGHT*
Aloe (p. 28)
Amaryllis (p. 29)
Anthurium (p. 31)
Asparagus fern (p. 32)
Banana plant (p. 36)
Bird-of-paradise (p. 37)
Bougainvillea (p. 38)
Burro's-tail (p. 39)
Calamondin orange (p. 41)
Calla lily (p. 42)
Chenille plant (p. 44)
Christmas cactus (p. 45)
Chrysanthemum (p. 45)
Coleus (p. 46)
Columnea (p. 47)
Creeping fig (p. 49)
Crocus (p. 50)
Croton (p. 51)
Crown-of-thorns (p. 51)
Cymbidium (p. 53)
Devil's-backbone (p. 53)
Dragon tree** (p. 55)
Echeveria (p. 56)
Firecracker flower (p. 60)
Flowering maple (p. 62)
Freesia (p. 63)
Fuchsia (p. 63)
Gardenia (p. 64)
Geranium (p. 65)
German ivy (p. 65)
Gloxinia (p. 66)
Grape ivy (p. 67)
Haworthia (p. 68)
Hibiscus (p. 69)
Hyacinth (p. 70)
Hydrangea (p. 71)
Ixora (p. 73)
Jade plant (p. 74)

Jerusalem cherry (p. 74)
Kalanchoe (p. 76)
Kangaroo vine (p. 77)
Lady's-slipper (p. 79)
Lantana (p. 80)
Lemon tree (p. 80)
Lily-of-the-valley (p. 81)
Lipstick plant (p. 82)
Living-stones (p. 82)
Madagascar jasmine (p. 83)
Mammillaria (p. 85)
Milkbush (p. 85)
Ornamental pepper (p. 90)
Oxalis (p. 90)
Paper-white narcissus (p. 91)
Passionflower (p. 92)
Peacock plant (p. 93)
Podocarpus (p. 99)
Poinsettia (p. 101)
Polka-dot plant (p. 101)
Portulacaria (p. 102)
Purple-passion vine (p. 103)
Rieger begonia (p. 105)
Rosary vine (p. 105)
Shrimp plant (p. 109)
Snake plant** (p. 109)
Starfish flower (p. 112)
Strawberry begonia (p. 112)
Streptocarpus (p. 113)
String-of-beads (p. 114)
Swedish ivy** (p. 114)
Sweet potato (p. 115)
Tulip (p. 119)
Umbrella plant (p. 119)
Venus's-flytrap (p. 120)
Vriesea** (p. 120)
Wandering Jew (p. 121)
Wax begonia (p. 122)
Wax plant (p. 122)

Yucca (p. 124)
Zebra plant (p. 124)

MEDIUM LIGHT
Achimenes (p. 27)
Aechmea (p. 27)
African violet (p. 28)
Amazon lily (p. 30)
Angel-wing begonia (p. 30)
Arrowhead vine** (p. 31)
Aucuba** (p. 32)
Avocado (p. 33)
Azalea (p. 33)
Baby's-tears (p. 34)
Balfour aralia (p. 34)
Bamboo palm (p. 35)
Bird's-nest fern** (p. 37)
Boston fern (p. 38)
Brake fern (p. 39)
Butterfly palm (p. 40)
Caladium (p. 40)
Camellia (p. 42)
Cast-iron plant** (p. 43)
Chinese evergreen** (p. 44)
Coffee tree (p. 46)
Corn plant (p. 48)
Creeping charlie (p. 49)
Cryptanthus (p. 52)
Cyclamen (p. 52)
Devil's ivy (p. 54)
Dieffenbachia** (p. 54)
Easter lily (p. 55)
English ivy** (p. 57)
European fan palm (p. 58)
False aralia (p. 59)
Fiddleleaf fig (p. 59)
Fishtail palm (p. 60)
Flame violet (p. 61)
Guzmania (p. 68)

Holly fern** (p. 70)
Impatiens (p. 72)
Iron-cross begonia** (p. 73)
Kaffir lily (p. 75)
Kentia palm** (p. 79)
Lady palm** (p. 79)
Lily-of-the-Nile** (p. 81)
Maidenhair fern** (p. 84)
Ming aralia (p. 86)
Monkey-puzzle (p. 86)
Moses-in-a-boat (p. 87)
Moth orchid (p. 88)
Nerve plant (p. 89)
Norfolk Island pine (p. 89)
Parlor palm** (p. 92)
Pellionia** (p. 94)
Peperomia** (p. 94)
Persian-shield** (p. 95)
Persian violet** (p. 96)
Philodendron** (p. 97)
Piggyback plant** (p. 98)
Pleomele** (p. 98)
Pocketbook flower (p. 99)
Ponytail** (p. 102)
Prayer plant** (p. 103)
Rex begonia (p. 104)
Rubber plant** (p. 106)
Sago palm (p. 107)
Schefflera (p. 107)
Screw pine (p. 108)
Spathiphyllum** (p. 110)
Spider plant** (p. 111)
Staghorn fern (p. 111)
Swiss-cheese plant** (p. 116)
Ti plant (p. 116)
Tree ivy** (p. 117)
Tuberous begonia (p. 118)
Waffle plant (p. 121)
Weeping fig (p. 123)

*The plants in this category need high light at certain stages of development for best growth or flowering. Many of them also thrive in medium light. Note that high light in winter is comparable to medium light the rest of the year. See page 11 for details on light.
**These plants prefer high or medium light, but will tolerate low light (see page 11). Keep in mind, though, that low light often retards bloom in flowering plants. It can affect color, shape, size, and number of leaves in foliage plants.

GIFT HOUSEPLANTS

African violet (p. 28)
Amaryllis (p. 29)
Azalea (p. 33)
Chrysanthemum (p. 45)
Crocus (p. 50)
Cyclamen (p. 52)

Cymbidium (p. 53)
Easter lily (p. 55)
Gloxinia (p. 66)
Jerusalem cherry (p. 74)
Pocketbook flower (p. 99)
Poinsettia (p. 101)

SCENTED HOUSEPLANTS

Easter lily (p. 55)
Freesia (p. 63)
Gardenia (p. 64)
Geranium (some) (p. 65)
Hyacinth (p. 70)

Lemon tree (p. 80)
Lily-of-the-valley (p. 81)
Madagascar jasmine (p. 83)
Paper-white narcissus
  (p. 91)

Houseplants for Different Decorating Needs

CLIMBING
Arrowhead vine (p. 31)
Bougainvillea (p. 38)
English ivy (p. 57)
German ivy (p. 65)
Grape ivy (p. 67)
Kangaroo vine (p. 77)
Madagascar jasmine (p. 83)
Passionflower (p. 92)
Philodendron (p. 97)
Sweet potato (p. 115)

HANGING
African violet (some) (p. 28)
Arrowhead vine (p. 31)
Baby's-tears (p. 34)
Burro's-tail (p. 39)
Creeping charlie (p. 49)
English ivy (p. 57)
Fuchsia (p. 63)
German ivy (p. 65)
Grape ivy (p. 67)
Philodendron (p. 97)
Piggyback plant (p. 98)
Rosary vine (p. 105)
Shrimp plant (p. 109)
Spider plant (p. 111)

Staghorn fern (p. 111)
Strawberry begonia (p. 112)
String-of-beads (p. 114)
Swedish ivy (p. 114)
Sweet potato (p. 115)
Wandering Jew (p. 121)

LARGE OR TREELIKE
Avocado (p. 33)
Balfour aralia (p. 34)
Bamboo palm (p. 35)
Banana plant (p. 36)
Butterfly palm (p. 40)
Camellia (p. 42)
Coffee tree (p. 46)
Corn plant (p. 48)
Croton (p. 51)
Dieffenbachia (p. 54)
Dragon tree (p. 55)
European fan palm (p. 58)
False aralia (p. 59)
Fiddleleaf fig (p. 59)
Fishtail palm (p. 60)
Gardenia (p. 64)
Hibiscus (p. 69)
Hydrangea (p. 71)
Jade plant (p. 74)
Jerusalem cherry (p. 74)

Kentia palm (p. 79)
Lady palm (p. 79)
Lemon tree (p. 80)
Milkbush (p. 85)
Ming aralia (p. 86)
Monkey-puzzle (p. 86)
Norfolk Island palm (p. 89)
Parlor palm (p. 92)
Pleomele (p. 98)
Rubber plant (p. 106)
Sago palm (p. 107)
Schefflera (p. 107)
Screw pine (p. 108)
Snake plant (p. 109)
Swiss-cheese plant (p. 116)
Ti plant (p. 116)
Tree ivy (p. 117)
Umbrella plant (p. 119)
Weeping fig (p. 123)
Yucca (p. 124)

SMALL OR TABLETOP
African violet (p. 28)
Angel-wing begonia (p. 30)
Aucuba (p. 32)
Baby's-tears (p. 34)
Cast-iron plant (p. 43)
Coleus (p. 46)

Creeping charlie (p. 49)
Crocus (p. 50)
Devil's-backbone (p. 53)
Devil's ivy (p. 54)
Freesia (p. 63)
Lady's-slipper (p. 79)
Peperomia (p. 94)
Polka-dot plant (p. 101)
Purple-passion vine (p. 103)
Strawberry begonia (p. 112)
Venus's-flytrap (p. 120)
Waffle plant (p. 121)
Wax begonia (p. 122)
Zebra plant (p. 124)

COLORFUL FOLIAGE
Caladium (p. 40)
Coleus (p. 46)
Croton (p. 51)
Nerve plant (p. 89)
Peacock plant (p. 93)
Polka-dot plant (p. 101)
Prayer plant (p. 103)
Purple-passion vine (p. 103)
Rex begonia (p. 104)

Easy-Care Houseplants

Aechmea (p. 27)
African violet (p. 28)
Aloe (p. 28)
Angel-wing begonia (p. 30)
Arrowhead vine (p. 31)
Asparagus fern (p.32)
Aucuba (p. 32)
Baby's-tears (p. 34)
Cast-iron plant (p. 43)
Chinese evergreen (p. 44)
Coleus (p. 46)
Creeping charlie (p. 49)
Devil's-backbone (p. 53)
Devil's ivy (p. 54)
Dieffenbachia (p. 54)
English ivy (p. 57)
German ivy (p. 65)
Grape ivy (p. 67)
Haworthia (p. 68)
Iron-cross begonia (p. 73)

Jade plant (p. 74)
Kangaroo vine (p. 77)
Living-stones (p. 82)
Mammillaria (p. 85)
Milkbush (p. 85)
Pellionia (p. 94)
Peperomia (p. 94)
Philodendron (p. 97)
Polka-dot plant (p. 101)
Rubber plant (p. 106)
Schefflera (p. 107)
Snake plant (p. 109)
Spider plant (p. 111)
Starfish flower (p. 112)
Strawberry begonia (p. 112)
Swedish ivy (p. 114)
Swiss-cheese plant (p. 116)
Ti plant (p. 116)
Vriesea (p. 120)
Wandering Jew (p. 121)

Houseplants and Kids

FUN TO GROW
Avocado (from pit) (p. 33)
Banana plant (with patience) (p. 36)
Lemon tree (from seed) (p. 80)
Piggyback plant (p. 98)
Spider plant (p. 111)
Starfish flower (p. 112)
Sweet potato (p. 115)
Ti plant (p. 116)
Venus's-flytrap (p. 120)

DANGEROUS
Azalea (p. 33)
Bird-of-paradise (p. 37)
Caladium (p. 40)
Dieffenbachia (p. 54)
English ivy (p. 57)
Geranium (some) (p. 65)
Hyacinth (p. 70)
Hydrangea (p. 71)
Jerusalem cherry (p. 74)
Lily-of-the-valley (p. 81)
Milkbush (p. 85)
Philodendron (p. 97)
Poinsettia (p. 101)

Unusual Houseplants

Banana plant (p. 36)
Bird-of-paradise (p. 37)
Bougainvillea (p. 38)
Ornamental pepper (p. 90)

Passionflower (p. 92)
Shrimp plant (p. 109)
Staghorn fern (p. 111)
String-of-beads (p. 114)

Houseplants
A TO Z

THE PAGES THAT FOLLOW PRESENT MORE THAN
190 PLANTS, EACH DIFFERENT IN COLOR, FORM,
AND SCENT. ALL ARE STANDOUTS IN THEIR OWN
WAY, IDEALLY SUITED FOR A SPECIAL PURPOSE IN
THE HOME AND A SPECIAL PLACE IN THE HEART.

Achimenes

Aechmea (opposite and above)

ACHIMENES (uh-KIM-uh-neez)

Achimenes species
Magic flower, monkey-faced pansy, orchid pansy, widow's-tears

Ideal for hanging baskets, achimenes rarely grows more than 12 inches high. Its tubular flowers come in a rainbow of colors.

LIGHT Expose to medium (bright indirect) light of east or west window. Grows well if under artificial light 16 hours per day.

WATER Keep soil evenly moist during active growth. Dry out slowly at season's end. Keep dry during storage.

TEMPERATURE Maintain temperatures of at least 65 degrees during early growth. Increase temperatures to the 80s during active growth. During storage, maintain temperatures in the 50s. Avoid cold at all times.

COMMENTS Plant rhizomes 2 inches apart and ¾ inch deep in African violet soil (1 rhizome per inch of pot opening). Feed every 14 days with dilute solution. Reduce and finally stop watering as leaves yellow. Store pot in cool, dry spot. Repot in spring to start new growth. Propagate by stem cuttings in spring, rhizome division or scales (on rhizomes) when repotting, or seed in midwinter.

AECHMEA (EEK-mee-uh)

Aechmea fasciata (fash-ee-AY-tuh)
Living-vase, urn plant

Aechmea forms a rosette of stiff leaves up to 20 inches tall and nearly as wide. Blue flowers cap a spike of pink bracts (leaves that simulate blooms).

LIGHT Expose to medium (bright indirect) light. Avoid full sun. But don't let light get too dim because plant needs strong light to flower.

WATER Keep leaves filled with water at all times. Mist frequently. Raise humidity.

TEMPERATURE Maintain average temperatures. Never let temperature go below 60 degrees.

COMMENTS Plant in shallow pot with orchid mix. Fertilize mix and leaves with dilute solution several times a year. Propagate by offsets.

AFRICAN VIOLET

Saintpaulia ionantha
(saint-PAUL-ee-yuh eye-oh-NAN-thuh)

African violet forms delightful clusters of flowers above a green rosette of hairy leaves.

LIGHT Expose to medium (bright indirect) light. Avoid full sun. Grows well if under artificial light 14 to 18 hours per day.

WATER Keep soil moist. Use tepid water; cold water spots leaves. Raise humidity.

TEMPERATURE Maintain high temperatures for best growth. Tolerates average temperatures. Avoid cold drafts.

COMMENTS Plant in shallow plastic pot with African violet mix. Fertilize regularly with dilute solution. Remove spent flowers and yellow leaves. Propagate by division when the crown forms more than one plant, or by leaf cuttings or seed.

African violet (miniature and standard)

ALOE (A-loh)

Aloe vera (VAIR-uh)
Burn plant, first-aid plant, medicinal aloe, unguentine cactus

Thick, fleshy leaves give aloe its distinctive cactus-like look. A striking foliage plant, aloe may occasionally bloom indoors. Many species other than *Aloe vera* are available.

LIGHT Place in high light (southern exposure); medium (bright indirect) light is OK. Plant needs intense light to bloom indoors. Grows well if under artificial light 16 hours per day.

WATER Let soil dry out considerably, but not completely, between thorough waterings. Overwatering causes root rot. Water less in winter.

TEMPERATURE Allow temperatures to climb into 80s during the day, but provide a drop of 10 degrees at night. Temperatures as low as 50 degrees at night are fine in winter.

COMMENTS Use soil that drains freely. Feed monthly during spring and summer. Move gradually into full sun outdoors in the summer to give plant the full light and warmth it needs. Propagate by cuttings, division, offsets, or seed.

Aloe

AMARYLLIS (am-uh-RIL-is)

Hippeastrum (hip-ee-AS-trum) species

A large bulb, amaryllis grows a stout stem and straplike leaves. It's a stunning winter or spring bloomer, producing clusters of lilylike flowers in a variety of colors, depending on species.

LIGHT Keep in dark during dormancy. Place in medium (bright indirect) light of east window during flowering and high light after flowering.

WATER Let soil dry during dormancy. Barely moisten to induce growth; keep evenly moist during active growth.

TEMPERATURE Maintain average temperatures during growth and low 40s during dormancy.

COMMENTS Set bulb half exposed in a 6-inch pot. Water lightly in midwinter to induce growth. After bulb sprouts, increase watering. Stake stem. Cut stem back to 2 inches after bloom. Water and feed for leaf growth. Stop both in early fall to initiate dormancy. Repot every three years in late fall. Propagate by bulb division (pull off the offsets at the side of the bulb when repotting) or seed (maintain temperatures above 68 degrees).

Amaryllis (left and above)

Amazon lily

AMAZON LILY

Eucharis grandiflora
(YOU-kuh-ris gran-di-FLOH-ruh)

Amazon lily is a stunning plant with fragrant white blossoms and large, attractive leaves.

LIGHT Expose to medium (bright indirect) light.

WATER Keep soil evenly moist except during winter, when it should be kept a little drier. Raise humidity.

TEMPERATURE Maintain temperatures of 68 degrees or higher for sprouting bulbs and above 60 degrees for mature plants.

COMMENTS Plant bulbs ½ inch deep. To ensure good bulb development, allow flowering only twice a year, pinching buds at other times. Propagate by offsets or seed. Maintain temperatures of 80 to 85 degrees for proper seed germination.

ANGEL-WING BEGONIA
(buh-GOH-nyuh)

Begonia coccinea (kok-SIN-ee-uh)

Angel-wing begonia gets its name from the shape of its leaves, which grow on stems that reach several feet in length if not pinched back. The plant forms clusters of flowers from spring to fall when conditions are ideal.

LIGHT Place in medium light. Bright east or west window is ideal. Avoid full sun, which pales leaves. Good light is essential for bloom.

WATER Allow soil surface to dry out between thorough waterings. Overwatering causes leaves to drop. Water less in fall and winter during dormancy. Mist regularly or set on a tray filled with moist pebbles.

TEMPERATURE Maintain average temperatures during active growth; provide low 60s in winter dormancy. Never allow to chill or freeze.

COMMENTS Place in small, shallow pot. Too large a pot retards bloom. Pot up only when rootbound. Pinch back to keep plant compact and bushy. Feed every 14 days with dilute solution during active growth. Propagate by stem cuttings.

Angel-wing begonia

ANTHURIUM (an-THUR-ee-um)

Anthurium species
Flamingo flower, painter's palette, pigtail plant, strap flower, tailflower

Waxy, brilliant, heart-shaped flowers (spathes) appear almost unreal above anthurium's attractive foliage. Always buy anthurium already in flower. Blooms last up to 12 weeks. Getting the plant to rebloom is difficult under average house conditions, but it's worth a try.

LIGHT Place in high light except during flowering; then, provide medium light. Full sun may damage bloom.

WATER Keep soil evenly moist. Maintain high humidity (up to 80 percent). Mist frequently with tepid water and set on a tray filled with pebbles and water, or double-pot, filling the space between the pots with moist sphagnum moss.

TEMPERATURE Maintain temperatures of 72 degrees or higher during the day and 10 degrees lower at night.

COMMENTS Use a growing medium high in an organic matter such as moss, fiber, bark, or peat. Feed at least once every four weeks with a dilute solution. Propagate by tip cuttings (vining varieties), offshoots (must have roots), or seed.

ARROWHEAD VINE

Syngonium podophyllum
(sin-GO-nee-um poh-doh-FIL-um)
or *Nephthytis* (nef-THY-tis) species
African evergreen, trileaf wonder

Arrowhead vine is a tropical trailing plant with foliage color and markings that vary by variety. It gets its name from the arrowhead shape of its leaves. Easy to grow, arrowhead vine thrives in hanging baskets or when supported by a stake.

LIGHT Place in medium light for best growth. Tolerates low light. Grows well if under artificial light 12 to 16 hours per day. Keep bulb 12 to 18 inches above the plant.

WATER Keep the soil moist, not soggy, at all times. Plant grows easily in water. Mist to maintain high humidity. If plant is grown on moss stick, keep moss moist at all times.

TEMPERATURE Maintain temperatures of at least 60 degrees, preferably close to 68 degrees.

COMMENTS Use soil high in organic matter. Let plant get pot-bound. Clean leaves often, but avoid leaf polishes. Give foliage a bath or wash in a warm shower occasionally. Feed with a dilute solution at least monthly in spring and fall, less often at other times. Pick off dry, yellow, or withered leaves. Pinch off growing tips regularly to encourage bushiness. Propagate by rooting the pinchings.

Anthurium

Arrowhead vine

31

ASPARAGUS FERN (uh-SPARE-uh-gus)

Asparagus species
Lace fern

The several species of asparagus that are commonly called asparagus fern are not really ferns at all, but they have the same graceful look as true ferns and are ideal for hanging baskets or broad shelves.

LIGHT Place in high light (full sun) during fall and winter. Give a southeastern exposure in spring and summer.

WATER Keep soil evenly moist. Mist daily. Raise humidity.

TEMPERATURE Maintain average temperatures. Never allow temperatures to drop below 50 degrees at night.

COMMENTS Cut back regularly for good appearance. New growth emerges rapidly. Feed monthly during active growth and much less the rest of the year. Propagate by division or from the little black seeds produced by the berries.

AUCUBA (AH-kew-buh)

Aucuba japonica (juh-PAH-ni-kuh)
Gold-dust plant, Japanese laurel

Gold-dust plant is a bold, durable plant with large, leathery leaves that have characteristic blotches of gold.

LIGHT Expose to medium (bright indirect) light. Tolerates low light.

WATER Keep the soil evenly moist, but not soggy. Mist daily to increase humidity.

TEMPERATURE Maintain temperatures in the low 70s in summer. Provide cooler temperatures in winter, with a 20-degree drop at night. Can withstand occasional freezing.

COMMENTS Plant aucuba in a large container to allow it room to grow into a small shrub. Pinch off growing tips to create bushy growth. Hard pruning is best done in late winter before active growth. Propagate by stem cuttings from half-ripened (firm, newer) wood, sections of root 1 to 2 inches long, or seed.

Asparagus fern

Aucuba

Avocado

Azalea

AVOCADO

Persea americana
(PUR-see-uh uh-meh-ruh-KAN-uh)
Alligator pear

Easy to grow from a pit, the avocado tree forms a canopy of elliptical green leaves. With proper care, it can last for years.

LIGHT Expose to medium (bright indirect) light. Move outdoors in summer in partial shade.

WATER Keep soil evenly moist. Leaf tips curl and turn brown if roots dry out. Mist frequently.

TEMPERATURE Maintain temperatures in the 80s for best growth. Plant tolerates average temperatures.

COMMENTS To start an avocado plant, first remove the pit from a ripe avocado. Let dry out; remove brown papery skin. Cut ¼ inch from the bottom (fat end). Push in three toothpicks equidistant around middle of pit. Set atop a water-filled jar, with the fat end of the pit resting in the water and the toothpicks on the jar's rim. Pot the pit when roots form. Pinch off the growing tip (light red stalk) at 8 inches. Feed regularly.

AZALEA (uh-ZAIL-ee-uh)

Rhododendron (roh-duh-DEN-drun) species

Given proper care, azalea—a popular gift plant—will produce brilliant blossoms year after year.

LIGHT Expose to medium (bright indirect) light. Summer outdoors in shade.

WATER Keep soil moist at all times during active growth. Mist.

TEMPERATURE Maintain cool temperatures (40s at night) to induce buds. Provide cooler-than-average temperatures, if possible, once in bloom.

COMMENTS Repot after flowering. Add fresh acidic peat moss. Feed with acid fertilizer every 14 days. Stop feeding as soon as buds form. Plant needs low temperatures, little water, medium light, and no fertilizer until January. Increase temperature and water to force new bloom. Propagate by stem cuttings taken from new growth in July, or by ground layering or seed anytime.

Baby's-tears

Balfour aralia

BABY'S-TEARS

Soleirolia soleirolii
(so-luh-ROH-lee-uh so-luh-ROH-lee-eye)
Angel's-tears, Corsican carpet plant, Corsican-curse, Irish moss, Japanese moss, mind-your-own-business

Baby's-tears forms a dense mat of light green threads. It has a delicate, almost frail, appearance and looks best displayed in a shallow pot. It's sometimes listed as *Helxine soleirolii*.

LIGHT Place in medium light (east or west window). Avoid placing too close to window.

WATER Keep soil evenly moist. Mist daily with tepid water. Raise humidity.

TEMPERATURE Maintain average temperatures. Avoid cold drafts.

COMMENTS Plant in a shallow pot with sand mixed into the growing medium. Prune to any desired shape. The plant may die back under less-than-ideal conditions, but it will regenerate if trimmed. Propagate by stem cuttings or division.

BALFOUR ARALIA
(BAL-for uh-RAIL-ee-uh)

Polyscias balfouriana
(poh-LIS-ee-us bal-FOR-ee-an-uh)

A woody plant, balfour aralia is grown for its foliage and unusual shape. Related varieties vary in height, but rarely grow more than 20 feet tall. All have a striking texture.

LIGHT Place in medium (indirect) light. Tolerates full sun for several hours a day.

WATER Keep moist at all times. Mist daily. Raise humidity.

TEMPERATURE Maintain temperatures as high as 80s during the day and not less than 62 degrees at night. Avoid drafts.

COMMENTS Plant in a large container; a redwood tub works well. Fertilize every 14 days with a mild solution during active growth. Clean leaves monthly with warm water. Water and feed less during winter. Propagate by root division, stem cuttings, or air layering.

Bamboo palm

BAMBOO PALM

Chamaedorea erumpens
(kam-ee-DOR-ee-uh ee-RUM-penz)

Bamboo palm is one of the best palms for indoor use because it grows no taller than 5 feet. It also costs less than other species. Its name comes from the rich, lush, bamboolike stems it sprouts.

LIGHT Expose to medium (indirect) light or filtered sun. Avoid full sun, which may pale the fronds.

WATER Keep soil evenly moist. Mist with tepid water.

TEMPERATURE Maintain high temperatures for best growth. Tolerates average temperatures. Avoid cold drafts.

COMMENTS Keep plant root-bound. During active growth, feed monthly with a dilute acid fertilizer. Do not overfertilize. Keep foliage clean. Remove dead or yellow leaves.

Banana plant

BANANA PLANT

Musa (MEW-zuh) species

Banana is an enjoyable—if offbeat—houseplant. *Musa nana* (*Musa cavendishii* or *Musa acuminata*) or *Musa velutina* is best suited to growth indoors. Do not expect fruit under average conditions.

LIGHT Expose to medium (bright indirect) light during early growth and high light (full sun) as first leaf forms. Set outside in summer; move gradually to full sun. Protect leaves from wind.

WATER Keep soil constantly moist. Mist daily. Raise humidity.

TEMPERATURE Maintain temperatures in 80s for best growth. Average temperatures OK.

COMMENTS Buy plants in spring. Or start from seed in midwinter. Nick seed's hard coating with nail file before soaking for 24 hours in warm water. Plant seed directly in a large tub. Use rich soil. Keep it moist but not soggy. During germination, keep soil temperature at 75 to 85 degrees. Germination takes two to 12 months. Feed often once growing. Clean leaves monthly. Propagate by the offsets that form after 13 to 20 months.

Bird-of-paradise

Bird's-nest fern

BIRD-OF-PARADISE

Strelitzia reginae (stri-LIT-zee-uh ree-JY-nee)

Bird-of-paradise is a spectacular, but extremely slow-growing, plant best suited to tub culture. It's noted for spearlike leaves and unusual flowers.

LIGHT Place in high light (full sun) during fall and winter, and medium (bright indirect) light in spring and summer.

WATER Allow soil surface to dry out between thorough waterings. Water a little less in fall and winter. Mist frequently.

TEMPERATURE Maintain average temperatures. Avoid cold drafts.

COMMENTS Fertilize regularly during active growth, less often in fall and winter. Remove damaged leaves or spent blossoms. Pot up when plant rises on its roots as if on stilts. Propagate by rhizome division after flowering, offsets, or seed (may take three to 10 years to flower). Use fresh seed.

BIRD'S-NEST FERN

Asplenium nidus (as-PLEE-nee-um NY-dus)

Bird's-nest fern forms a rosette of brilliant fronds somewhat similar to banana plant leaves. The plant may grow as large as 6 feet across in time.

LIGHT Expose to medium (bright indirect) light, preferably with an eastern exposure. Tolerates low light.

WATER Allow soil surface to dry out between thorough waterings. Keep humidity high by double-potting. Mist older plants daily.

TEMPERATURE Maintain temperatures below 75 degrees during the day and above 50 degrees at night. Plant likes cool temperatures.

COMMENTS Use a porous growing medium with lots of peat, vermiculite, or coarse sand. Grow in clay pots, if possible; they breathe, keeping roots cool. Feed every 14 days with extremely mild solution during active growth. Clean foliage with frequent, but gentle, baths. Pot up when severely root-bound (roots grow slowly). Avoid insecticides. Propagate by division in March or by spores when plants are mature.

BOSTON FERN

Nephrolepis exaltata 'Bostoniensis'
(neh-FROL-uh-pis eks-awl-TAY-tuh)

Boston fern boasts pale green leaves that can stretch 3 feet (less in more-compact varieties). Hanging baskets with built-in saucers provide ideal growing conditions as well as dramatic appeal.

LIGHT Place in medium (indirect) light of east window.

WATER Allow soil to dry out between thorough waterings. Mist with tepid water. Raise humidity, especially in warm weather from March through September.

TEMPERATURE Maintain temperatures of no more than 75 degrees during the day and no less than 50 degrees at night. Avoid drafts.

COMMENTS Grow in clay pots; they breathe, keeping roots cool. Use porous soil rich in organic matter: compost, leaf mold, or peat. Pot up only when severely root-bound. Feed every two to three weeks with extremely mild fertilizer. Avoid insecticides. Don't confuse brown spots on undersides of leaves, which contain spores, with insects. Propagate by division in early spring, or by runners (threads off side of plant) or spores when mature.

Boston fern

BOUGAINVILLEA (boo-gun-VIL-yuh)

Bougainvillea species
Paper flower

Profuse papery blossoms in hot colors accent bougainvillea, an otherwise unattractive vining plant.

LIGHT Set in high light (southern exposure). Move gradually into full sun outdoors in summer.

WATER Allow soil surface to dry between thorough waterings. Water more frequently during bloom. Reduce watering during dormancy.

TEMPERATURE Maintain high temperatures for best growth. Plant tolerates average temperatures. Place next to a south-facing wall outdoors in summer. Bring indoors before frost.

COMMENTS Support with stakes. Prune to desired shape or into a standard (tree form); responds well to drastic cutting back. Leaves fall during dormancy, but new leaves form immediately. Feed heavily during spring and summer. Avoid repotting; plant will drop leaves and stop blossoming if roots are disturbed. Instead, replace soil on surface of pot each spring before active growth. Plant blossoms when days are short. Propagate by seed anytime or 6-inch cuttings taken from newer growth (not stiff, old wood) in spring.

Bougainvillea

Brake fern

BRAKE FERN

Pteris (TEER-is) species
Table fern

Brake fern has feathery, almost soft foliage. Cultural needs vary by species, but the following suggestions apply to most.

LIGHT Expose to medium (bright indirect) light of east window. Too much sun pales fronds.

WATER Allow soil surface to dry out between thorough waterings. Mist as often as possible. Keep humidity very high.

TEMPERATURE Maintain temperatures in the low 70s during the day and mid 50s at night.

COMMENTS Grow in clay pots, if possible; they breathe, keeping roots cool. Use porous growing medium high in organic matter. Feed every three weeks with mild fertilizer in spring and summer, less often in fall and winter. Pot up only when badly root-bound. Propagate by division or spores.

BURRO'S-TAIL

Sedum morganianum
(SEE-dum mor-gun-ee-AY-num)

Burro's-tail is one of the finest trailing plants for indoor gardening. As it matures, it forms pendulous silvery blue-green tassels. Pinkish red flowers appear at the tips of mature plants under ideal conditions.

LIGHT Place in high light year-round, preferably in south window indoors or direct sun outdoors. Augment low light with artificial light of up to 18 hours per day.

WATER Allow soil to dry out between thorough waterings. But do not let soil stay dry too long, or leaves will shrivel and drop. Do not mist.

TEMPERATURE Maintain average temperatures. Tolerates from low 50s to low 80s. Avoid cold drafts or frosty windowpanes.

COMMENTS Keep out of traffic; bumps cause leaves to drop. Use porous soil. Fertilize no more than once every four months during active growth. Propagate by seed or leaf cuttings in spring. Let cuttings dry for five days before planting.

Burro's-tail

Butterfly palm

BUTTERFLY PALM

Chrysalidocarpus lutescens
(kri-sal-i-doh-KAR-pus loo-TESS-enz)
Areca palm

Butterfly palm forms a cluster of nonbranching, yellowish stems or canes with numerous fronds or leaves.

LIGHT Expose to medium (bright indirect) light. Avoid full sun.

WATER Allow soil surface to dry out between thorough waterings. Mist daily.

TEMPERATURE Maintain temperatures below 80 degrees during the day and above 60 degrees at night. Avoid cold drafts.

COMMENTS Pot up two sizes every two to three years. Use deep pots. Fertilize lightly each month, giving slightly heavier doses during active growth. Wash dust from leaves each month by giving the plant a gentle shower. Propagate by seed or division in spring.

CALADIUM (kuh-LAY-dee-um)

Caladium species
Fancy-leaved caladium

Grow caladium for its translucent foliage in shades of pink, red, silver, and white.

LIGHT Expose to medium (bright indirect) light. Avoid full sun.

WATER Keep soil evenly moist during active growth; stop watering during dormancy.

TEMPERATURE Maintain high temperatures for best growth. Tolerates average temperatures.

Caladium

COMMENTS Start tubers in March in soil medium rich in peat or other organic matter. Place tubers, bumpy side up, 1 inch or less below soil surface. Keep soil moist, not soggy, and above 70 degrees until tips emerge. Provide bottom heat for better germination. Tubers rot when soil temperature is low. Fertilize every 14 days with dilute solution. Avoid cold drafts. Water less in late fall and allow leaves to die back. Store at 50 to 55 degrees. Repot and start watering again after several months of dormancy. Propagate by dividing tubers when repotting; or cut tubers into portions with at least one eye, then plant them just as you would a potato (dust with fungicide and set them, cut side down, 1 inch deep).

Calamondin orange

CALAMONDIN ORANGE
(kal-uh-MON-din)

Citrus mitis (SIT-rus MY-tis)

A delightful, ornamental tree, calamondin orange produces tangerine- or orangelike fruit even when small. Flowers smell sweet.

LIGHT Place in high light (full sun) year-round. Move into full sun outdoors in summer over a period of 14 days.

WATER Allow soil surface to dry out between thorough waterings. Mist. Raise humidity.

TEMPERATURE Maintain temperatures in the low 70s during the day and no less than 50 degrees at night. Avoid frost at all costs.

COMMENTS Fertilize monthly in spring and summer. Prune to desired height and shape in spring. Keep leaves clean. Propagate by cuttings taken from newer growth (not old, hard stem) in early spring. Propagation by seed is difficult and is not recommended for home gardeners.

CALLA LILY (KAL-uh)

Zantedeschia (zan-tuh-DES-kee-uh) species

Calla lily is an elegant flowering houseplant with blooms (spathes) that last many weeks. White-, pink-, and yellow-bloomed varieties are available.

LIGHT Place in high light (full sun) during fall and winter and medium light (morning sun) during spring and summer. Move out of direct sun when flowering so bloom lasts longer.

WATER Keep evenly and completely moist at all times. Mist frequently. Raise humidity.

TEMPERATURE Maintain temperatures in the mid-70s during the day and no lower than 50 degrees at night.

COMMENTS Plant tubers 1 inch deep in early spring or late fall in 6-inch or larger clay pots. Plant one tuber in a 6-inch pot, more in larger pots. Use soil rich in organic matter. Leave enough room at top of pot to add 1 inch more soil later. Keep moist and warm. As growth appears, fill in the pot with an additional inch of soil. Feed every two to three weeks. When flowers fade and foliage turns yellow, stop feeding and watering. Remove the tubers from the pot, cut off the foliage, and shake the soil from the roots. Propagate by dividing tubers at this time. Repot. Resume light watering to stimulate new growth. Also propagate by offsets or seed.

CAMELLIA (kuh-MEEL-yuh)

Camellia species

Camellia provides large, colorful, and perfectly formed blooms on rich green foliage. Unfortunately, it thrives only in cool houses or greenhouses.

LIGHT Expose to medium (bright indirect) light. The morning light of an eastern exposure is ideal. Put outside in the shade each summer.

WATER Keep constantly moist during spring and summer. Reduce watering during fall and winter. To provide highest humidity possible, mist daily if indoors; spray daily with a hose if outdoors.

TEMPERATURE Maintain temperatures of no higher than 68 degrees during the day and in low 40s at night (tough to provide in most homes).

Calla lily

COMMENTS Use soil that retains moisture but drains freely. Best soil has a high-acid, peat-moss content. Replace soil if compacted. Buds form in late summer or fall for winter bloom (camellia is one of the few plants that bloom during dormancy). Reduce water and fertilizer during bloom. When buds form, remove all but one bud per cluster, or poke nail into bud so it shrivels and dries up. Do not confuse slender growth buds with fat flower buds. Remove spent blossoms. Repot only after flowering. Prune at same time to control height and create bushier plant. May be trained into a standard (tree form). Use acid fertilizer every two weeks during active growth. Propagate by ground layering or cuttings taken from half-ripened wood (when wood loses its pink tinge). Dust cuttings with hormone powder; place in moist rooting medium. To stimulate root growth, which may take three months or more, keep cuttings warm with bottom heat and moist with plastic covering.

CAST-IRON PLANT

Aspidistra elatior
(as-puh-DIS-truh ee-LAY-tee-or)
Barroom plant

Cast-iron plant, a slow grower, can take considerable neglect, but it responds to good care with shiny dark leaves, which often are used in floral arrangements. Variegated varieties also are sold.

LIGHT Expose to medium (bright indirect) light for best growth, especially of variegated varieties. Tolerates low light. Avoid full sun, which pales leaves. Grows well if under artificial light 14 hours per day.

WATER Keep evenly moist, but never soggy. Plant tolerates drying of soil surface. Mist daily.

TEMPERATURE Maintain temperatures below 80 degrees during the day. For dark green varieties, never let temperatures drop below 50 degrees at night. For variegated varieties, never below 60 degrees at night.

COMMENTS Feed monthly with dilute solution during active growth. Fertilize variegated forms less often to retain leaf color. Clean leaves monthly. Because plant resents being disturbed, repot or pot up only when absolutely necessary. Propagate by division in spring. Each rhizome should have at least two leaves attached to it.

Camellia

Cast-iron plant

Chenille plant

CHENILLE PLANT (shuh-NEEL)

Acalypha hispida (a-kuh-LYE-fuh HIS-pid-uh)
Philippine-medusa, red-hot cattail

Chenille plant's soft, fuzzy, furlike flowers bloom over a long period. Getting the plant to rebloom, though, is difficult because it demands extremely high humidity.

LIGHT Place in high light (southern exposure) during fall and winter, and medium light in spring and summer. Prefers morning sun. Needs high light for good flowering.

WATER Keep soil evenly moist. Mist leaves with tepid water; never mist flowers. Raise humidity as high as possible.

TEMPERATURE Maintain temperatures in the 80s for best growth. Tolerates temperatures of 70s during the day and 60s at night.

COMMENTS Feed monthly with dilute solution. Cut back plant each spring to maintain compact size and renew growth. Propagate by 4-inch stem cuttings taken during active growth.

CHINESE EVERGREEN

Aglaonema (ag-lay-oh-NEE-muh) species
Painted drop-tongue, spotted evergreen

Chinese evergreen is one of the most durable foliage plants. Leaf color and size vary by variety.

LIGHT Place in medium light of east or west window. Tolerates low light, but variegated forms lose coloration under such conditions.

WATER Keep soil moist at all times. Water a little less in fall and winter. Mist as frequently as possible. Keep humidity high by placing on a tray filled with moist pebbles.

TEMPERATURE Maintain temperatures in the low 80s during the day and no less than the low 60s at night.

COMMENTS Grow in soil or water. Because plant likes being pot-bound, pot up only when roots fill entire pot. Feed monthly with a weak solution. Clean foliage monthly with tepid water. Propagate by air layering, division, stem cuttings (root in sand), or tip cuttings (will root in water).

Chinese evergreen

CHRISTMAS CACTUS

Schlumbergera bridgesii
(shlum-BER-jer-uh BRIJ-zee-eye)

Christmas cactus often is confused with Thanksgiving or Easter cactus. All have arching foliage with brilliant flowers that cascade in whorls of colored petals. And all require care similar to that outlined below. Their leaves do vary in shape.

LIGHT Place in high light (southern exposure) in fall and winter, and medium light in spring and summer. Keep dark 12 hours a day from October 1 until bloom.

WATER Keep soil evenly moist except in fall; then, let it dry between waterings. Raise humidity.

TEMPERATURE Maintain temperatures in the low 70s during the day and no lower than low 50s at night, except between October 1 and bloom. Then, keep temperatures below 53 degrees all day.

COMMENTS Feed less in fall. *Never* move or turn plant once it's in bloom; it will drop buds and stop flowering. Propagate by stem cuttings or seed.

Christmas cactus

CHRYSANTHEMUM
(kreh-SAN-thuh-mum)

Dendranthema grandiflora
(den-DRAN-thuh-muh gran-di-FLOH-ruh)
Mum

Mums are popular gift plants. For longest enjoyment, buy plants with more buds than flowers. Getting plants to reflower in the home is difficult.

LIGHT Place in medium light while plant is in flower and high light during vegetative growth. Place in complete darkness 14 hours per day in fall to encourage bud formation.

WATER Keep soil moist except after flowering; then, water less. Mist.

TEMPERATURE Maintain temperatures of 50 to 60 degrees during day and in the 40s at night.

COMMENTS Cut stems back to 4 inches after bloom. Reduce watering until new growth emerges. Then, water and feed regularly. Pinch tips for bushy growth or prune into a standard (tree form). Propagate by stem cuttings.

Chrysanthemum

COFFEE TREE

Coffea arabica (KOFF-ee-uh uh-RAB-i-kuh)
Arabian coffee

Coffee tree is an exotic indoor plant with dark green leaves. The tree takes several years to mature and rarely produces flowers or berries (beans) indoors. Flowers are white, fragrant, and well worth the careful attention you'll have to pay to misting, temperature, and fertilizing.

LIGHT Expose to medium (strong indirect) light for best growth. Avoid full sun.

WATER Keep soil almost wet in summer. Mist often during heat waves. Raise humidity.

TEMPERATURE Maintain temperatures in the low 70s during the day and high 60s at night. Keep temperatures the same year-round for best results. Avoid drafts.

COMMENTS Feed monthly with acid fertilizer during active growth. Feed less often in fall and winter. Regularly and gently clean leaves. Prune to any shape. Propagate by using unroasted beans as seed (provide bottom heat), or by taking tip cuttings from main upright stems of mature plants.

Coffee tree

COLEUS (KOH-lee-us)

Coleus species
Flame nettle, painted leaves, painted nettle

Coleus is a sumptuous foliage plant with richly colored, velvety leaves. It thrives indoors with minimal care.

LIGHT Place in high (bright) light for full foliage coloration. Vary location to control color.

WATER Keep the soil moist. Mist frequently to raise humidity.

Coleus

Columnea

COLUMNEA (kuh-LUM-nee-uh)

Columnea species
Goldfish plant, Norse fire plant

With its trailing stems and splashy tubular flowers, columnea is ideal draped over a pot on a table or in a hanging basket. Related to gloxinia, it's somewhat finicky, but is worth the effort. Grow the hybrids for longer bloom and extra hardiness.

LIGHT Expose to high light (southern exposure) during winter and medium (bright indirect) light the rest of the year. Set outside in filtered—not full—sun. Grows well if under artificial light 16 hours per day.

WATER Keep evenly moist except during dormancy. Use tepid water to avoid spotting leaves. To aid bud formation, water less in fall, stopping completely for one month. Some growers stop watering twice a year—once in summer and once in winter—to get two seasons of bloom. Raise humidity to prevent leaves and buds from dropping.

TEMPERATURE Maintain average temperatures. If plant does not form buds, lower temperatures into 50s or 60s. Avoid drafts.

COMMENTS Plant in a soil rich in organic matter: peat, compost, leaf mold, or rotted manure. Feed with a mild fertilizer every 14 days during active growth. Prune to retain shape and increase bushiness, but only after flowering. Propagate by seed (provide warm and humid conditions), or by tip cuttings taken after flowering.

TEMPERATURE Maintain average temperatures, preferably between 60 and 68 degrees.

COMMENTS Feed every 14 days during active growth. Pinch to create bushy plants. Remove all blossoms. Prune into a standard (tree form), if desired. Propagate by cuttings rooted in water or peat-based rooting medium, or by seed (needs light to germinate). Cuttings will create plants similar to the parent plant; seeds are less predictable.

Corn plant

CORN PLANT

Dracaena fragrans 'massangeana'
(druh-SEE-nuh FRAY-granz mah-sun-jee-AY-nuh)

A tough plant, corn plant gets its name from the shape and color of its leaves. It occasionally produces creamy, scented blossoms indoors, but only under ideal conditions.

LIGHT Place in medium (indirect) light for best growth. Plant, though, tolerates many different light conditions. In low light, variegated leaves often lose striping but remain a lush green.

WATER Allow soil surface to dry between thorough waterings. Mist regularly.

TEMPERATURE Maintain temperatures of 60 to 75 degrees. Avoid drafts.

COMMENTS Plant in rich soil that retains moisture but drains freely. Plant likes being pot-bound. Pinch off the growing tip to create a bush. If a tree shape is preferred, let the growing tip be. Clean leaves monthly with a damp sponge dipped in tepid water. Propagate by cuttings (tip or stem), air layering, or seed.

CREEPING CHARLIE

Pilea nummulariifolia
(PY-lee-uh num-mew-lay-ree-eye-FOH-lee-uh)

Creeping charlie is a good choice for hanging baskets. It has light green leaves on reddish stems. Note that the garden creeping charlie, which is often thought of as a weed, is a completely different plant: *Nepeta hederacea*.

LIGHT Place in medium light (bright indirect or filtered sun). Move plant to find preferred spot.

WATER Keep soil evenly moist at all times. Mist frequently. Raise humidity.

TEMPERATURE Maintain average temperatures, preferably 65 to 75 degrees.

COMMENTS Fertilize lightly every 14 days. Pinch off growing tips to create bushy plants and keep growth under control. Propagate by stem cuttings or root division. For fullest look, curl long stems around the plant and pin each node into the soil. Stems will root where they are pinned to soil.

CREEPING FIG

Ficus pumila (FY-kus PEW-mi-luh)
Climbing fig, creeping rubber plant

Unlike most of its cousins, this plant is ivylike and trailing. It will creep up the damp wall of a greenhouse or a moss stick inside the home. It also is attractive in hanging baskets.

LIGHT Expose to high light (full sun) in fall and winter, and medium (bright indirect) light in spring and summer. Provide filtered light outdoors, although plant can tolerate shade. Grows well if under artificial light for 16 hours per day.

WATER Allow soil surface to dry between thorough waterings. Mist daily. If grown on a moss stick, mist the moss; the plant clings to the stick with aerial roots.

TEMPERATURE Maintain temperatures of 60 to 75 degrees.

COMMENTS Feed every 14 days with a mild solution. Wash foliage monthly. Cut back to control size or vary shape. Propagate by 6-inch cuttings taken in spring.

Creeping charlie

Creeping fig

Crocus

CROCUS (KROH-kus)

Crocus species

Many crocus varieties do extremely well when potted and forced for winter color. The yellow or saffron varieties are not recommended. Use only one variety per pot since varieties bloom at different times (the basket above contains five small pots of two different varieties).

LIGHT Keep bulbs in a dark spot for 12 weeks, then move into medium to high light. Plant outside in location with medium to high light.

WATER Keep soil moist during initial cooling. Water frequently while plant is growing. When leaves yellow, reduce and then stop watering. Let bulbs go dormant for a time, then plant outside and start watering again.

TEMPERATURE Maintain temperature of 35 to 45 degrees for 12 weeks. Raise temperature to 50 to 60 degrees until buds form. Once buds form, move to higher temperatures to stimulate flowering. Keep warm after flowering to promote leaf growth and increase bulb size for outdoor bloom.

COMMENTS Buy the largest bulbs available, three to four months before desired bloom time. Each bulb contains a flower bud. Mix extra peat and 1 teaspoon of bonemeal into soil. Plant seven bulbs to each shallow, 5-inch bulb pot (more in larger pots). Bulb tips should just stick out of soil. Water and place in cool, dark spot for several months. Keep soil damp. As bulbs sprout, move into cool, bright spot until buds form. Then move into warmer spot to force bloom. After bloom, cut off stalks to prevent seed formation. Stop feeding and watering when leaves yellow. Let plants rest. When weather warms, plant bulbs outside.

CROTON (KROH-tun)

Codiaeum variegatum
(koh-dee-EE-um vair-ee-uh-GAY-tum)
**Garden croton, joseph's coat,
variegated laurel**

Croton is an unusual, but striking, houseplant.
The color combinations in its leaves are remark-
able and extremely bright. The shape of its leaves
varies considerably among the different varieties.

LIGHT Place in high light (southern exposure) during winter. Provide medium light rest of
year. Lots of light is the key to full color.

WATER Keep soil evenly moist. Dry soil
causes leaves to drop. Mist daily.

TEMPERATURE Maintain average temperatures. Avoid all drafts, which cause leaf drop.

COMMENTS Feed monthly from spring to
early fall, less during winter. Pinch growing tips to
create a bushy, instead of a single-stemmed, plant.
Propagate by air layering when plant looks
frumpy, seed sown in March or April, or cuttings
taken from March through June.

CROWN-OF-THORNS

Euphorbia splendens
(you-FOR-bee-uh SPLEN-denz)

Unusual because of its curving stems, crown-of-
thorns should be used as a living sculpture. Leaves
drop occasionally, but the red flowers (bracts) that
appear at the tips of spiny branches are attractive.

LIGHT Place in high light (south exposure).

WATER Allow soil surface to dry out between
thorough waterings. Water less in fall when the
plant is dormant. Use tepid water because cold
water causes leaves and blossoms to drop.

TEMPERATURE Maintain an evenly warm
temperature. Avoid hot and cold drafts.

COMMENTS Plant in sandy soil rich in organic matter. Prune to desired shape. Feed during
flowering, usually January through March. The
pale leaves drop periodically, which is normal.
Propagate by tip cuttings or sections of root 1 to 2
inches long taken after flowering.

Croton

Crown-of-thorns

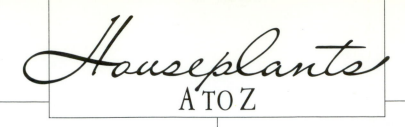

CRYPTANTHUS (krip-TAN-thus)

Cryptanthus species
Earth-star

Cryptanthus forms a rosette of colorful leaves. Flowers appear occasionally, but they're hidden by the leaves in some varieties.

LIGHT Expose to medium (bright indirect) light.

WATER Keep cup at center of leaves filled at all times. Change water about every 10 days. Keep growing medium moist. Mist frequently.

TEMPERATURE Maintain temperatures of 60 to 75 degrees. Avoid cold drafts.

COMMENTS Plant in a shallow container in orchid potting mix. Spray dilute fertilizer on leaves and growing medium monthly. Encourage flowering in a mature plant by placing it in a plastic bag with a ripening apple. The fruit gives off ethylene gas, which stimulates blossoming. Avoid pesticides. Propagate by offsets.

Cryptanthus

CYCLAMEN (SY-kluh-men)

Cyclamen species
Poor man's orchid

Cyclamen's upright stems carry heart-shaped leaves and graceful, waxy flowers. Some varieties may bloom for months. This gift plant can be difficult to get to rebloom.

LIGHT Expose to medium light (east).

WATER Keep evenly moist. To avoid crown rot, do not water leaves directly. Water less after bloom. Keep barely moist when foliage dies back and plant is dormant. Resume watering when leaves resprout. Mist daily. Raise humidity.

TEMPERATURE Maintain temperatures no higher than 68 degrees during the day, with a drop of 10 degrees at night. Avoid all drafts.

COMMENTS Fertilize weekly during active growth. Remove yellow leaves. Repot after leaves die back. Propagate by corm divison during dormancy. Or, if you're patient, try seed. Germination takes 21 days at 68 degrees; flowering takes another 18 months.

Cyclamen

CYMBIDIUM (sim-BID-ee-um)

Cymbidium hybrids

Cymbidium orchid is grown for its stunning winter blossoms on grassy stems.

LIGHT Place in high light (full sun) in winter and medium to high light the rest of the year. Place outdoors in summer if possible. Needs three weeks of short days (12 hours of darkness) in fall to stimulate new bloom.

WATER Keep evenly moist, but not soggy. Never allow medium to dry out.

TEMPERATURE Maintain average temperatures. Needs 55 degrees or below during the three weeks of short days prior to blooming.

COMMENTS Pot in special orchid mix. Fertilize with dilute solution every two weeks during active growth. Propagate by division, leaving parent plant with four stems.

DEVIL'S-BACKBONE

Pedilanthus tithymaloides
(ped-uh-LAN-thus tith-uh-muh-loh-EYE-deez)

With zigzag stems and pointed leaves, devil's-backbone makes an ideal vertical accent plant. Its leaves often drop during the fall, and the plant occasionally bears red birdlike flowers.

LIGHT Expose to high light (southern exposure). Grows well if under artificial light 14 hours per day. Leaves lose color in low light.

WATER Keep evenly moist. Leaves drop if soil dries out. Reduce watering in fall and early winter. Mist as often as possible.

TEMPERATURE Maintain temperatures of 55 to 80 degrees.

COMMENTS Prune to control size and legginess. When pruning, wear rubber gloves to prevent irritation from sap. Feed every 14 days. Propagate by division, or by cuttings rooted in water or moist rooting medium.

Cymbidium

Devil's-backbone

DEVIL'S IVY

Epipremnum aureum
(ep-i-PREM-num AW-ree-um)
Golden pothos, pothos

Often mistaken for philodendron, devil's ivy has heart-shaped leaves with varied markings. Let it climb a bark support or trail from a hanging basket. It was formerly known as *Scindapsus aureus*.

LIGHT Expose to medium (bright indirect) light. Avoid full sun. Move according to season. Good light helps plant retain bright markings.

WATER Allow soil to dry out between thorough waterings. If plant is staked, keep stake moist by misting. Clean foliage monthly.

TEMPERATURE Maintain high temperatures for best growth. Tolerates average temperatures. Avoid cold drafts.

COMMENTS Use soil mixed with coarse, sterile sand and peat moss. Plant also grows in water. Pinch for bushiness. Propagate by division or cuttings. Use portions of stem with aerial roots.

Devil's ivy

DIEFFENBACHIA (dee-fen-BAHK-ee-uh)

Dieffenbachia species
Dumb cane, mother-in-law plant, tuftroot

Dumb cane gets its name from toxic leaves and stems that cause numbness in the tongue when eaten. The plant rarely blooms indoors.

LIGHT Place in medium (indirect) light. Tolerates low light.

WATER Allow soil to dry out between thorough waterings. Mist daily. Prefers humidity, but tolerates dryness. If too dry, leaf tips brown.

TEMPERATURE Maintain high temperatures (into 80s) during the day, if possible, and temperatures no less than low 60s at night. Avoid drafts.

COMMENTS Feed every 14 days during active growth with dilute solution. Remove dead leaves. Clean leaves with tepid water. Propagate by tip cuttings, stem cuttings, suckers, or air layering. Cut the plant back to its base when it gets leggy. Use the upper portion as a tip cutting and the cane for stem cuttings, then let the stump regenerate.

Dieffenbachia

Dragon tree

Easter lily

DRAGON TREE

Dracaena marginata
(druh-SEE-nuh mar-jin-AY-tuh)
Madagascar dragon tree

Sturdy and adaptable, dragon tree may take years to mature.

LIGHT Place in high light (full sun) in winter and medium (bright indirect) light the rest of the year. Tolerates low light.

WATER Allow soil to dry between thorough waterings. Mist daily in warm seasons, more often in hot weather, and never in cool weather. Increased humidity prevents brown leaf tips.

TEMPERATURE Maintain high temperatures in day for best growth. Average temperatures OK.

COMMENTS Pot up in spring if needed. Feed every 14 days during active growth. Clean leaves monthly. Propagate by air layering, stem cuttings, or seed (keep soil at 86 degrees).

EASTER LILY

Lilium longiflorum (LIL-ee-um lon-ji-FLOH-rum)

Easter lily is noted for its trumpetlike flowers and heavenly scent.

LIGHT Expose to medium (bright indirect) light until plant dies back. Store bulb in dark until new growth starts. Then move into low to medium light. Move to medium light when blooming starts.

WATER Allow soil surface to dry between thorough waterings. Water less after flower dies, eventually letting plant go dry. Water lightly to spur new growth.

TEMPERATURE Maintain temperatures in the 60s, especially during flowering. Store bulb at 40 to 45 degrees until new growth starts.

COMMENTS When plant dies back, cut stalk, clean bulb, and store in cool, dark place. In August, plant bulb deep in a pot, barely covering it; add soil as growth occurs. Place in dark, cool spot. Water lightly. When growth starts, move into warmth and light. When bloom occurs 115 days later, move to brighter light. When foliage dies back, restart cycle. Propagate by seed or bulb scales.

Echeveria

ECHEVERIA (ek-uh-VEER-ee-uh)

Echeveria species
Numerous common names by species

Echeveria produces finely colored and thick-leaved rosettes, and sends up spikes of tubular blossoms. Numerous varieties are sold, all of which are easy to grow.

LIGHT Place in high light (southern exposure). Move outdoors during summer to increase exposure. Grows well if under artificial light 16 hours per day.

WATER Let soil dry out between thorough waterings March through September. Water just enough to stop leaves from drying the rest of the year. Too much water causes root rot. Prefers dry air; do not mist or raise humidity in any way.

TEMPERATURE Maintain temperatures of up to 80 degrees during the day and no lower than 50 degrees at night.

COMMENTS Add lots of coarse, sterile sand to soil. Feed lightly April through July; avoid feeding in fall and winter when the plant is dormant. Older plants may lose bottom leaves, which is normal. Propagate by offsets in spring or leaf cuttings of upright species, normally taken in fall.

ENGLISH IVY

Hedera helix (HED-uh-ruh HEE-liks)

One of the most popular and easy-to-grow house-plants, English ivy splashes deep green from containers or hanging baskets. It also can be trained to wind up supports. Many varieties are available.

LIGHT Expose to medium (bright indirect) light. Plant tolerates low to high light conditions. Vary location to find the best spot. Grows well if under artificial light 14 hours per day.

WATER Keep evenly moist. Mist to clean foliage and raise humidity. Prefers higher humidity, but tolerates dry conditions.

TEMPERATURE Maintain average temperatures. For best growth, keep temperatures cool (to 55 degrees) at night.

COMMENTS Feed every 14 days during active growth. Will grow in either water or soil. Prune to obtain length desired and force branching. Excellent for arrangement into topiary shapes. Just fold chicken wire into any desired form, then fill with moist sphagnum moss. Insert ivy cuttings. Wash with tepid water frequently to deter red spider mites. Propagate by division or stem cuttings.

English ivy

EUROPEAN FAN PALM

Chamaerops humilis (KAM-ee-rops HEW-mi-lus)
Dwarf fan palm

European fan palm spreads out with a number of arching trunks and stiff fronds to form foliage fans. It usually stays bushy.

LIGHT Expose to medium (bright indirect) light. Plant tolerates low light if all other conditions are favorable. Avoid full sun, which can burn the leaves. Grows well if under artificial light for 16 hours per day. Foliage color changes with age and light exposure; vary location to get just the right tone.

WATER Keep evenly moist, allowing soil surface to dry out between waterings. Avoid soggy soil around roots. Place pot on saucer filled with pebbles and water to raise humidity.

TEMPERATURE Maintain average temperatures. Avoid cold drafts.

COMMENTS Use porous soil for good drainage. Plant in deep pots. When potting up, provide a pot two sizes bigger. Pot up every spring until plant reaches desired size. During active growth, fertilize monthly with extremely mild solution. Do not overfeed. Wipe leaves with damp cloth. Propagate by seed, providing high bottom heat; or propagate by cutting suckers from base of plant.

European fan palm

FALSE ARALIA (uh-RAIL-ee-uh)

Dizygotheca elegantissima
(diz-ee-go-THEE-kuh el-ee-gan-TIS-i-muh)
Threadleaf

One of the most pleasing indoor foliage plants, false aralia has lacy, graceful foliage.

LIGHT Expose to medium (bright indirect) light. Avoid full sun. Grows well if under artificial light 16 hours per day.

WATER Allow soil to dry out between thorough waterings. Mist daily if possible. Raise humidity to deter red spider mites.

TEMPERATURE Maintain temperatures in the low 60s for best growth. Plant tolerates average temperatures.

COMMENTS Plant in porous soil for good drainage. Fertilize every 14 days during active growth. Sponge leaves once a month with tepid water. Don't apply leaf oils. If lower leaves drop as plant ages, cut it back to start new growth. Propagate by tip cuttings, root division, or air layering.

False aralia

FIDDLE-LEAF FIG

Ficus lyrata (FY-kus ly-RAY-tuh)

Fiddle-leaf fig produces shiny, leathery leaves in the shape of a violin (hence, the name).

LIGHT Expose to medium (bright indirect) light. Vary location by season to provide right conditions. Avoid full sun. Grows well if under artificial light 16 hours per day.

WATER Allow soil surface to dry out between thorough waterings. Because plant likes above-normal humidity, mist whenever possible. Place plant on tray filled with moist pebbles.

TEMPERATURE Maintain high temperatures for best growth. Plant tolerates temperatures of 60 to 75 degrees.

COMMENTS Use porous soil to avoid sogginess around roots. Feed every 14 days during active growth. Wipe dust from leaves regularly with a moist cloth. Avoid all leaf polishes. Propagate by stem cuttings or air layering when plant loses its lower leaves and looks straggly.

Fiddle-leaf fig

FIRECRACKER FLOWER

Crossandra infundibuliformis
(kros-SAN-druh in-fun-dib-yuh-luh-FOR-mis)

Firecracker flower produces salmon to orange-red, tubular flowers atop glossy, dark green foliage. Often beginning to bloom when only a few inches tall, this plant rarely grows more than 1 foot tall.

LIGHT Place in high light (southern exposure) in winter and medium (bright indirect) light the rest of the year. Needs bright light to flower well. Summer outdoors in partial shade. Grows well if under artificial light 14 hours a day.

WATER Keep soil evenly moist, but never soggy, using tepid water. Mist as frequently as possible; use tepid water to avoid spotting leaves. Likes high humidity. If dry, leaves may curl.

TEMPERATURE Maintain average temperatures. Avoid all drafts.

COMMENTS Pot up each February if root-bound. Feed weekly with dilute solution during active growth. Prune to desired shape in spring. Propagate by seed (a tough task) or tip cuttings taken in spring when pruning plant.

Fishtail palm

Firecracker flower

FISHTAIL PALM

Caryota mitis (kair-ee-OH-tuh MY-tis)

Easy to grow, fishtail palm is a striking foliage plant with deep green, leathery leaves that resemble fishtails.

LIGHT Expose to medium (bright indirect) light. Avoid full sun. Grows well if under artificial light 16 hours per day.

WATER Allow soil surface to dry out between thorough waterings. Mist daily, especially during hot weather. Raise humidity.

TEMPERATURE Maintain average temperatures. Tolerates no lower than high 50s at night. Avoid cold drafts.

COMMENTS Pot up two sizes on a regular basis during early years of growth. Use deep pots. Let older plants get root-bound. Feed with dilute mixture during active growth. Do not overfeed. Clean leaves monthly with damp cloth. Propagate by division, seed (soil temperature in 80s), or suckers.

Flame violet

FLAME VIOLET

Episcia (i-PISH-ee-uh) species

A splendid, tropical trailing plant, flame violet produces creeping stems that are covered with small plantlets. In spring and summer, brilliant and abundant blossoms appear. Dozens of varieties are available.

LIGHT Expose to medium (bright indirect) light at all times. Move plant to find just the right environment. Proper light is crucial for an abundant, lengthy blooming period. Grows well if under artificial light 16 hours per day.

WATER Keep soil evenly moist. Never let it get soggy, nor allow it to dry out completely. To avoid spotting, do not get water on leaves. Mist around plant, but not on it. Needs lots of humidity. Set on tray or saucer filled with pebbles and water.

TEMPERATURE Maintain high temperatures for best growth. Tolerates average temperatures. To avoid killing plant, never let temperatures drop below 55 degrees.

COMMENTS Use African violet mix with lots of organic matter. Let plants trail from shelf or hanging basket. Feed every 14 days during active growth. Prune to control growth. Propagate by leaf cuttings, runners, seed, or tip cuttings.

Flowering maple (below and below right)

FLOWERING MAPLE

Abutilon (uh-BEW-ti-lon) species
Chinese-lantern, Indian mallow, parlor maple

Whether freestanding, trained to a support, or hanging from a basket, flowering maple boasts papery blossoms in an assortment of colors. The blossoms last much of the year under ideal conditions. Many varieties with a wide range of leaf shapes and colors exist.

LIGHT Place in high light (full sun) during winter and medium (bright indirect) light the rest of the year. Blooms poorly in low light. Place in shade outdoors in summer.

WATER Keep soil evenly moist. Mist daily. Prefers higher humidity.

TEMPERATURE Maintain temperatures into the 50s at night for best growth. Plant tolerates average temperatures.

COMMENTS Pot up regularly. Feed lightly and sporadically with low-nitrogen fertilizer. Pinch to retain shape, create bushiness, and spur more blooms. Remove yellow leaves daily to stimulate growth. Propagate by seed or tip cuttings.

FREESIA (FREE-zee-uh)

Freesia species

Place freesia, a forced bulb, near your bed to enjoy its scent at night. Blooms come in many colors.

LIGHT Place in darkness for 12 weeks in the fall, medium light during bud formation, and high light during bloom and leaf growth.

WATER Keep barely moist during initial root growth, evenly moist during bud formation, and very moist during bloom and leaf growth.

TEMPERATURE Maintain temperatures in the low 50s until buds form. Tolerates average temperatures once in bloom.

COMMENTS Plant corms ½ inch deep and 1 inch apart in shallow pots filled with porous soil in early fall. Keep barely moist, cool, and in darkness until growth starts. Move to cool spot with medium light to encourage budding. Feed and water regularly. Support with stakes. Bring into warmer room once in bloom; water well. Keep moist and well fed until foliage dies. Store pot on side in dry, cool spot until the next fall. Restart process. Propagate by seed or cormels from beside parent corm.

Freesia

FUCHSIA (FEW-shuh)

Fuchsia x hybrida (HIB-ri-duh)
Ladies'-eardrops

Upright or trailing, fuchsia produces spectacular bell-like blooms in a wide range of colors.

LIGHT Place in high light (full sun) in winter and medium (bright indirect) light rest of year.

WATER Keep evenly moist. Mist daily. Raise humidity, but provide good air circulation. Never let roots dry out. Water less during dormancy.

TEMPERATURE Maintain temperatures below 68 degrees during day and in low 50s at night for best growth. Tolerates average temperatures.

COMMENTS Feed every 14 days during active growth. Pinch tips for bushiness. Prune if leggy. Blooms develop near growing tips, so pinch and prune each spring to encourage new growth. Remove faded flowers. Drops leaves in late fall and winter. Propagate by tip cuttings taken in spring.

Fuchsia

Gardenia

GARDENIA (gar-DEEN-yuh)

Gardenia jasminoides (jas-min-oh-EYE-deez)
Cape jasmine

One of the more difficult flowering houseplants, gardenia is still worth the effort for its glossy green foliage and waxy, scented flowers.

LIGHT Place in high light (southern exposure) in winter and medium (bright indirect) light rest of year. Place outdoors in filtered light in summer. Expose to artificial light during gray periods.

WATER Keep soil evenly moist, but never soggy. Do not let soil around roots dry out. Mist daily with tepid water. Raise humidity as high as possible by using humidifier or double-potting.

TEMPERATURE Maintain temperatures in low 60s to encourage buds, but not below 70 degrees once buds form. Avoid cold drafts.

COMMENTS Use acid potting soil. Fertilize regularly, supplementing with iron chelate and 1 teaspoon of ammonium sulfate in 1 gallon of water. Pinch off buds after one flowering period when plant is still young. Remove spent blossoms. Prune to shape after flowering; may be trained into standard (tree form). Keep foliage clean. Propagate by cuttings taken from firm, new growth in late spring, or by seed anytime for some varieties.

GERANIUM (juh-RAIN-ee-um)

Pelargonium (peh-lar-GOH-nee-um) species

Many people throw their geraniums away after one season of bloom, which is a shame, since they're so easy to propagate from stem cuttings.

LIGHT Place in high light (southern exposure) during all seasons. During gray periods, expose to 14 hours of artificial light per day.

WATER Let soil dry out between waterings. Avoid soggy conditions, which can be fatal.

TEMPERATURE Maintain cool temperatures for best growth, especially at night (low 50s). Tolerates average temperatures.

COMMENTS Feed monthly with mild solution low in nitrogen; supplement with calcium. Prune to control size and create bushier plant. Prune into standard (tree form) over period of years. Propagate by stem cuttings or seed (difficult in some varieties). Start stem cuttings each year from favorite varieties and overwinter as smaller plants.

GERMAN IVY

Senecio mikanioides
(si-NEE-shee-oh my-kay-ni-oh-EYE-deez)
Parlor ivy, water ivy

Easy to grow and ideal for hanging baskets, German ivy has the same soft look as English ivy.

LIGHT Place in high light (southern exposure) during winter and medium (bright indirect) light rest of year. If possible, place outdoors during summer in filtered light.

WATER Let soil surface dry out between thorough waterings. Don't let soil around roots dry out; may be fatal. Mist daily. Keep humidity high.

TEMPERATURE Maintain temperatures into mid-50s at night for best growth. Tolerates average temperatures.

COMMENTS Pot up each February if rootbound. Use porous soil. Feed every 14 days during active growth; feed less in late fall and winter. Pinch growing tips continually to create bushiness. Remove leaves as they die. Propagate by tip cuttings rooted in water or moist rooting medium.

Geranium

German ivy

Gloxinia

GLOXINIA (gloks-IN-ee-uh)

Sinningia speciosa (si-NIN-jee-uh spee-si-OH-suh)

A regal plant, gloxinia boasts bell-shaped flowers in vivid colors and large, velvety leaves.

LIGHT Place in dark during dormancy. Move into medium (bright indirect) light when growth starts. Move to high light (full sun) in winter.

WATER Keep barely moist during dormancy. Keep evenly moist at all other times. Mist around plant when not dormant, keeping water off leaves to prevent spotting. Raise humidity.

TEMPERATURE Maintain cool temperatures (no lower than 50 degrees) during dormancy. At other times, provide high temperatures.

COMMENTS Plant tuber in spring in 6-inch pot with African violet mix. Set tuber round side down, with its tip barely above the soil. Water. Feed when buds form. Remove first few buds. When leaves die in fall, remove. Move plant to cool, dark place. Keep barely moist. Will sprout in four to 10 weeks. Move to light and warmth to restart cycle. Propagate by leaf or stem cuttings, offsets, seed, or tuber division.

GRAPE IVY

Cissus rhombifolia (SIS-us rom-bi-FOH-lee-uh)

Grape ivy is a fast-growing plant that's easy to care for. The furry tendrils are covered with clusters of sharp-toothed leaves.

LIGHT Place in high light (southern exposure) during winter and medium (bright indirect) light the rest of the year.

WATER Keep evenly moist at all times. Mist often. Prefers high humidity.

TEMPERATURE Maintain temperatures in high 50s at night for best growth. Tolerates average temperatures.

COMMENTS Provide support or hanging basket for best display. Feed every 14 days with mild solution. Clean foliage monthly. Prune ruthlessly to maintain shape and create a bushy plant. Propagate by rooting stem cuttings in water or a peat-based rooting medium.

Grape ivy

Guzmania

Haworthia

GUZMANIA (gooz-MAN-ee-uh)

Guzmania lingulata (ling-you-LAY-tuh)

Guzmania forms funnel-shaped rosettes of glossy, smooth leaves in various shades of green and red. The striking blooms may last for several months.

LIGHT   Place in medium (bright to bright indirect) light of east or west window.

WATER   Keep evenly moist and humid at all times. Fill rosette of leaves with water. Mist frequently; set pot on tray filled with moist pebbles.

TEMPERATURE   Maintain temperatures in high 70s, if possible. Average temperatures OK.

COMMENTS   Use light, porous growing medium. Spray medium and foliage with dilute fertilizer monthly during active growth. Plant often dies back after bloom, but forms offsets at its base. Plant offsets for a new brood of exotic bromeliads.

HAWORTHIA (hah-WURTH-ee-uh)

Haworthia species
Aristocrat plant, cushion aloe, pearl plant, star cactus, wart plant

Haworthia is a spiky-leaved plant that, because of resistance to drought and cold, is ideal for a bright windowsill. The many species available offer interesting, simple shapes, and are easy to grow.

LIGHT   Place in high light in winter and medium (bright to bright indirect) light the rest of the year. Set outside in partial shade in summer.

WATER   Allow soil to dry out between thorough waterings. Keep barely moist during winter rest period to avoid root rot.

TEMPERATURE   Maintain average temperatures during active growth. Let temperatures drop into high 50s during winter rest period. Plant tolerates temperatures into the low 40s.

COMMENTS   Add coarse, sterile sand to potting mixture to improve drainage. Repot at least once every two years, removing all dead roots. Feed with a dilute solution during active growth, but no more than once a year. Propagate by the offsets that form around the main leaf rosette or by leaf cuttings in spring and summer.

HIBISCUS (hy-BIS-kus)

Hibiscus rosa-sinensis (ROH-suh-sy-NEN-sis)
Chinese hibiscus, Chinese rose

A hibiscus plant will last for decades, producing papery blooms over a period of months each year. Blooms, however, will last no more than two days. Despite its showiness, hibiscus is one of the most reliable indoor flowering plants.

LIGHT Place in high light (southern exposure) in winter and medium (bright indirect) light the rest of the year. Place outdoors in summer.

WATER Keep soil evenly moist, especially during bloom. Raise humidity. High humidity and moist soil necessary to keep buds from dropping.

TEMPERATURE Maintain average temperatures. Avoid all drafts.

COMMENTS Prune back ruthlessly after flowering. May be summer or winter bloomer, depending on induced dormant period. Induce dormancy by watering less and stopping feedings. Feed every week during active growth. Propagate by seed or tip cuttings from new growth.

Hibiscus (left and above)

HOLLY FERN

Cyrtomium falcatum
(sur-TOH-mee-um fal-KAY-tum)
Japanese holly fern

Adaptable and easy to grow, holly fern has shiny, leathery fronds that resemble holly leaves.

LIGHT   Place in medium light of east window. Tolerates low light (northern exposure).

WATER   Keep evenly moist at all times with tepid water. Allow slight drying in winter. Mist with tepid water. Keep humidity high.

TEMPERATURE   Maintain temperatures of no higher than 75 degrees during the day and no lower than 50 degrees at night. Prefers cool.

COMMENTS   Feed with mild solution monthly. Remove yellow or damaged fronds. To fill with new fronds, cut plant back to soil line. Avoid insecticides. Do not confuse brown dots on leaves, which contain spores, with scale insects. Propagate by division in spring or spores when mature.

HYACINTH (HY-uh-sinth)

Hyacinthus orientalis
(hy-uh-SIN-thus or-ee-en-TAY-lis)

Hyacinth offers rich colors and a lovely scent when forced to bloom for indoor display.

LIGHT   Place in the dark during dormancy. Offer medium light during budding and bloom. Needs high light after bloom for good leaf growth and tuber formation.

WATER   Provide no water during dormancy. Water lightly to stimulate new growth. Water regularly during active growth.

TEMPERATURE   Maintain temperatures between 32 and 50 degrees during dormancy and not above 55 degrees during bud formation. Prefers cool temperatures during flowering, but tolerates average temperatures.

Holly fern

Hyacinth

Hydrangea

COMMENTS Buy the largest bulbs available. Because varieties bloom at different times, plant only one variety in each wide, shallow pot (planter at left, below, contains three individually potted varieties). Plant bulbs in fall no deeper than ¾ inch. Water; set in cool (40 degrees), dark place—a refrigerator works well—for eight to 12 weeks. Keep barely moist until growth starts, then water regularly. Move into medium light and temperatures no higher than 55 degrees until buds form. Just before bloom, move into warmer area, if desired. Water and fertilize regularly until blooms fade and leaves yellow. Provide high light after blooming. When leaves die back, stop watering. Remove leaves. Store bulbs in pot or remove. Store in cool, dry place. Restart cycle in fall. Propagate by potting bulblets formed on parent bulb.

HYDRANGEA (hy-DRAN-jee-uh)

Hydrangea macrophylla (mak-roh-FIL-uh)

Bell-shaped flower clusters are hydrangea's delight. Getting it to rebloom, though, is a challenge.

LIGHT Place in low light during dormancy. Place in high light before and during bloom; set in medium light the rest of the year. Place outdoors in summer.

WATER Keep barely moist during dormancy. Keep evenly moist rest of year. Never allow soil to dry out during growth and bloom. Mist daily except during dormancy. Prefers higher humidity.

TEMPERATURE Store plant at 45 degrees during dormancy. Raise temperature to no more than 55 degrees to encourage new growth, then to 60 degrees when leaves form. During and after bloom, maintain temperatures below 70 degrees during the day and into the low 60s at night.

COMMENTS To create new growth for future flowers, cut the plant back after bloom. Feed and water well as new growth forms. In fall, store in cool (45 degrees), dim area. Leaves will fall. Water just enough to keep soil moist. After Christmas, bring into light and maintain temperatures of no more than 55 degrees. Water normally. Mist stem with tepid water. As leaves form, feed and soak with supplement solution (1 ounce ammonium sulfate and 1 ounce iron sulfate in 2 gallons water). Increase temperature to 60 degrees until bloom. During bloom, never let temperatures exceed 70 degrees. Propagate by tip cuttings in spring.

IMPATIENS (im-PAY-shenz)

Impatiens wallerana (wall-er-AY-nuh)
Busy lizzy, patience plant, patient lucy

Impatiens is a bushy, delicate plant that blooms profusely in a wide range of colors. A popular bedding plant, impatiens does well indoors with proper care.

LIGHT   Place in medium (bright to bright indirect) light. Needs 14 hours of light for full bloom indoors. Augment with artificial light, if needed.

WATER   Keep evenly moist. Dry soil causes bud drop and flower loss. Raise humidity by placing on tray filled with moist pebbles.

TEMPERATURE   Maintain temperatures of 50 to 60 degrees, if possible. Tolerates average temperatures. Keep out of hot or cold drafts to avoid leaf drop and yellowing.

COMMENTS   Fertilize weekly with dilute solution during active growth. Pinch for bushiness, especially after bloom. Propagate by seed in late winter and early spring or stem cuttings anytime.

Impatiens

Iron-cross begonia

IRON-CROSS BEGONIA (buh-GOH-nyuh)

Begonia masoniana (muh-soh-nee-AY-nuh)

Iron-cross begonia gets its name from the cross shape that appears on each of its broad leaves. Because they're lovely as well as durable, this begonia and its relatives make superb foliage plants. Iron-cross begonia produces delicate pink and green blossoms in spring, but the flowers are insignificant compared to the foliage.

LIGHT Place in medium to high light during the winter and medium light the rest of the year. Tolerates low light. Grows well if under artificial light 14 hours per day.

WATER Allow soil to dry out slightly between thorough waterings. Mist daily. Raise humidity.

TEMPERATURE Maintain temperatures to low 60s at night for best growth. Plant tolerates average temperatures.

COMMENTS Feed weekly with mild solution during active growth. Pinch growing tips to control growth and to produce bushier plants. Propagate by rhizome division or seed.

IXORA (ik-SOAR-uh)

Ixora species
Flame-of-the-woods, jungle-flame, jungle geranium, star flower

Ixora resembles a miniaturized hydrangea. Of the many species in the ixora family, the most common is one with bright red flowers in clusters 4 to 6 inches wide. Its leaves are bronze when young and deep green when mature. A few species have scent.

LIGHT Place in high light (full sun) during winter and medium (bright indirect) light the rest of the year. Summer outdoors in filtered light.

WATER Keep evenly moist except in fall; then, water less. Mist daily. Needs high humidity.

TEMPERATURE Maintain temperatures into the 80s for best growth. Plant tolerates average temperatures.

COMMENTS Plant in acid, lime-free soil. Add iron if leaves turn yellow. Don't feed during fall. Reduce watering at same time. Resume normal watering and feeding at Christmas. Prune plant after dormancy. Pinch back regularly. To avoid jostling buds from plant, do not move it during bloom. Ixora usually flowers in spring or summer, but may bloom sporadically at other times. Propagate by tip cuttings taken in spring. Set pot with cuttings on heating pad or heating cable.

Ixora

JADE PLANT

Crassula argentea
(KRASS-yew-luh ar-JEN-tee-uh)
Chinese rubber plant

Jade plant looks like a miniature tree with thick, fleshy leaves. Under ideal conditions, old plants produce fragrant, star-shaped blossoms.

LIGHT Place in high light (southern exposure) during winter and medium (bright indirect) light rest of year. If you provide full sun at times other than winter, leaves will pale.

WATER Let soil dry out between thorough waterings. Soggy soil causes rot.

TEMPERATURE Maintain high temperatures for best growth. Tolerates average and below-average temperatures.

COMMENTS Feed every 14 days during active growth. Plant in sandy soil for best results. Clean leaves monthly with damp cloth. Pinch off growing tips for branching and compact growth. Keep older plants pot-bound to stimulate flowering. Propagate by stem or leaf cuttings, or seed.

Jade plant

JERUSALEM CHERRY

Solanum pseudocapsicum
(soh-LAY-num soo-doh-KAP-si-kum)

A small shrub favored at the holidays, Jerusalem cherry produces pretty but poisonous globes.

LIGHT Place in high light (southern exposure) during winter and medium (bright indirect) light the rest of the year.

WATER Keep evenly moist when actively growing and nearly dry during dormancy.

TEMPERATURE Maintain temperatures in the 50s at night for best growth. Tolerates average temperatures. Keep plant cool for two months during winter dormancy. Avoid cold drafts.

COMMENTS Feed every six weeks during active growth. Prune to control growth. Train into a standard (tree form). Allow to go dormant in January and February by withholding fertilizer, cutting back on water, and placing in cool (60 degrees) spot. Propagate by seed.

Jerusalem cherry

Kaffir lily

KAFFIR LILY (KAF-ur)

Clivia miniata (KLY-vee-uh min-ee-AY-tuh)

Related to amaryllis, the dramatic and exotic kaffir lily produces brilliant clusters of flowers above straplike leaves.

LIGHT Place in medium light of east window. Avoid full sun.

WATER Let soil dry out between thorough waterings. Water just enough to keep leaves alive during dormancy.

TEMPERATURE Maintain temperatures into the low 60s for best growth. Plant tolerates average temperatures.

COMMENTS Plant in large container. Add bonemeal to soil. Avoid replanting. If you do repot, remove any diseased or rotting sections of ropelike root. Feed weekly during active growth. *Never* move, even a little, once in bud. Cut off flowers after bloom. Let plant go dormant from October to January by withholding food and watering less. Propagate by offshoots in spring or division after flowering. Division retards bloom for two years.

KALANCHOE (kal-un-KOH-ee)

Kalanchoe blossfeldiana
(bloss-fel-dee-AY-nuh)
Christmas kalanchoe

Christmas kalanchoe boasts clusters of starlike flowers that stay in bloom night and day. Blossom colors include scarlet, orange, and yellow.

LIGHT Place in high light (southern exposure) for full flower color. Strictly control light conditions in fall (see below).

WATER Allow soil to dry out between thorough waterings. Water less during fall dormancy, but never allow leaves to wither.

TEMPERATURE Maintain cool temperatures for best growth. Tolerates average temperatures.

COMMENTS Feed every 14 days from spring to fall. Remove spent blossoms. Pinch back for more compact plant. Plant must have total darkness 14 hours a day for three to four weeks in the fall. Some insecticides kill this plant, so read labels carefully. Propagate by seed or tip or leaf cuttings.

KANGAROO VINE

Cissus (SIS-us) *antarctica*

An easy-care, quick-growing foliage plant, kangaroo vine has large, oval, shiny leaves. Either train up a support or display in a basket.

LIGHT Place in high light (southern exposure) in winter. Provide medium (bright indirect) light rest of year.

WATER Keep evenly moist except in fall and early winter. Then, water less. Do not let plant dry out. Mist as frequently as possible.

TEMPERATURE Maintain temperatures of 65 to 70 degrees during active growth. Provide three-month rest period during winter with temperatures from 50 to 55 degrees.

COMMENTS Prune when young for bushiness. During active growth, feed with mild solution every 14 days. Stop feeding in fall and early winter. Clean leaves regularly. Propagate by tip cuttings taken in spring.

Kangaroo vine

Lady palm

Kentia palm

KENTIA PALM (KEN-tee-uh)

Howea forsterana
(HOW-ee-uh for-ster-AY-nuh)

Slow growing and durable, kentia palm is probably the best palm for indoor culture.

LIGHT Expose to medium (bright indirect) light. Tolerates low light. Pales in full sun. Grows well if under artificial light 16 hours per day.

WATER Allow soil surface to dry out between thorough waterings. Water less in fall and early winter. Mist daily in normal weather, more often in hot weather. Raise humidity.

TEMPERATURE Maintain temperatures in the 80s for best growth. Tolerates average temperatures. Avoid all drafts.

COMMENTS Pot up in spring in deep pot. Use porous soil. Plant several in large pot for fuller look. Feed with mild solution spring to fall. Don't overfeed. Clean leaves often. Propagate by seed. Be aware, though, that plants take years to mature.

LADY PALM

Rhapis (RAY-pis) species
Slender lady palm

Rarely reaching more than 5 feet tall, lady palm looks best with numerous bamboolike stems. This plant is one of the best palms, but because of slow growth, it's expensive.

LIGHT Expose to medium (bright indirect) light. Avoid full sun. Tolerates low light. Grows well if under artificial light 16 hours per day.

WATER Allow soil to dry out between thorough waterings. Mist as often as possible, especially in hot weather. Raise humidity.

TEMPERATURE Maintain average temperatures. Never let temperature go above 75 degrees. Prefers cool temperatures at night. Avoid drafts.

COMMENTS Pot up each spring in deep pot until plant is desired size. Use porous soil. Feed mild solution monthly from March through October, but do not overfeed. Add iron to diet occasionally. Wash leaves monthly. Propagate by seed (provide bottom heat), or by suckers at plant base.

LADY'S-SLIPPER

Paphiopedilum (paf-ee-oh-PED-i-lum) species
Slipper orchid

Somewhat tricky to grow, lady's-slipper produces pouchlike blossoms once a year. Flowers last for months in good conditions.

LIGHT Place in high light in winter and medium (bright indirect) light the rest of the year. Eastern exposure is best.

WATER Keep growing medium constantly moist and humidity high. Don't let plant go dry.

TEMPERATURE Maintain average temperatures. Drop temperatures by 10 degrees at night.

COMMENTS Use orchid potting mix and shallow pot. Repot yearly to change medium. Feed every 14 days in spring and summer, and monthly in fall and winter. Propagate by division or seed.

Lady's-slipper

LANTANA (lan-TAN-uh)

Lantana camara (KAM-uh-ruh)
Shrub verbena, yellow sage

Lantana is versatile and free flowering. Its clusters of vibrantly colored flowers may last for several months. Display lantana in a hanging basket or train it into tree form for a stunning accent plant.

LIGHT Place in high light (southern exposure) year-round for best flowering.

WATER Allow soil surface to dry out between thorough waterings. Mist daily.

TEMPERATURE Maintain average temperatures, with drop of 10 degrees at night.

COMMENTS Fertilize weekly with mild solution during active growth. Cut back older plant to spur new growth. To train into standard (tree form), select and attach straight stem to stake. Remove lower leaves as plant matures. When plant reaches desired height, pinch growing tips. Top will form compact bush. Propagate by seed or tip cuttings. You can propagate anytime, but for best results, do so in September or February.

Lantana

LEMON TREE

Citrus limon (SI-trus ly-MOHN)

Lemon tree grows slowly indoors, but its scented white blossoms, fruit, and glossy green leaves make it an attractive plant.

LIGHT Place in high light (full sun) during winter and medium (bright) light the rest of the year. Summer outdoors, gradually exposing to bright light over a period of 14 days.

WATER Allow soil surface to dry out between thorough waterings. Mist daily.

TEMPERATURE Maintain cool temperatures (to low 50s) for best growth. Tolerates average temperatures. Keep cool during bloom, if possible.

COMMENTS Use an acid soil or acid fertilizer. Feed every 14 days during active growth. Wash leaves monthly. Prune ruthlessly to control size. Propagate easily by seed anytime or with difficulty from stem cuttings taken from firm, new growth in spring.

Lemon tree

LILY-OF-THE-NILE

Agapanthus (ag-uh-PAN-thus) species
African lily

Lily-of-the-Nile is admired for its lovely display of spherical flower clusters above straplike leaves.

LIGHT Place in high light (full sun) during winter and medium (bright) light the rest of the year. Tolerates low light.

WATER Keep soil evenly moist except during the dormancy that follows flowering; then, keep soil barely moist. Never allow soil to dry out.

TEMPERATURE Maintain temperatures of no higher than low 70s during day and in 50s at night. Tolerates even lower than 50 degrees.

COMMENTS Plant in a large, deep tub to prevent roots from breaking pot. Because plant likes being pot-bound, keep in same pot for years. Feed every 14 days with mild solution after flower stem appears. Propagate by seed anytime or by dividing the fleshy roots in February or March.

LILY-OF-THE-VALLEY

Convallaria majalis
(kon-vuh-LAIR-ee-uh muh-JAY-lis)

Lily-of-the-valley produces 6-inch plants with sweetly scented, bell-shaped flowers.

LIGHT Place in darkness or low light until growth appears, then medium (bright) light.

WATER Keep barely moist until new growth appears. Water regularly during active growth. Mist daily. Raise humidity.

TEMPERATURE Maintain temperatures of 70 degrees or lower at all times. Prefers cooler.

COMMENTS In fall, dig and clean pips (rootstocks), then place in refrigerator for 6 weeks. Or buy precooled pips. Pot 12 cooled pips in 5-inch pot, with buds just above soil. Place pot in dark for 10 days at 60 degrees. Keep soil moist, not soggy. As growth starts, bring into bright light at 70 degrees. Pips take 21 days from planting to bloom. After foliage dies, remove pips; store in cool, dry place. Plant outside in spring. Let pips grow outdoors for a year and a half before restarting process.

Lily-of-the-Nile

Lily-of-the-valley

LIPSTICK PLANT

Aeschynanthus (es-kuh-NAN-thus) species
Basket vine

Lipstick plant produces long vines with small tubular flowers, usually scarlet with yellow throats. Related species vary widely. Choose according to what most appeals to you: foliage, flowers, or scent.

LIGHT Place in high light (southern exposure) during winter and medium (bright indirect) light the rest of the year. Good light can extend bloom for months.

WATER Keep evenly moist at all times. Plant drops buds and leaves if dry. Mist early each day. Raise humidity.

TEMPERATURE Maintain temperatures in the 80s during the day for best growth. Plant tolerates average temperatures. Avoid cold drafts.

COMMENTS Use peat moss and osmunda as growing medium. Feed monthly with mild solution during active growth. After bloom, cut back to 6 inches. Plant will regenerate and produce many buds. Propagate by seed, ground layering, or tip cuttings (provide high humidity and warmth).

Lipstick plant

LIVING-STONES

Lithops (LITH-ops) species
Flowering-stones, mimicry plant, stoneface

Living-stones looks just like a small rock split down the middle. It rarely blooms indoors.

LIGHT Place in high light (southern exposure) year-round to better odds of bloom.

WATER Allow soil to dry out between thorough waterings. Water just enough in winter to keep leaves alive.

TEMPERATURE Maintain average temperatures. From 50 to 80 degrees OK.

COMMENTS Use porous, sandy soil. After planting, never repot or pot up. Do not feed. Propagate by seed in spring or by division of mature plants in early summer every three to four years.

Living-stones

Madagascar jasmine

MADAGASCAR JASMINE

Stephanotis floribunda
(stef-uh-NOTE-is flor-i-BUN-duh)
Floradora, wax-flower

When not full of fragrant, white tubular flowers, stephanotis still is attractive for its glossy, leathery leaves. The plant is tricky to grow, but worth a try. It's often used in bridal bouquets.

LIGHT Place in high light (full sun) as much as possible, especially in winter. Put outside in summer, gradually exposing to full sun.

WATER Keep moist at all times. Mist daily. Raise humidity. If too dry, buds and flowers drop. If plant is outside, spray daily with mist of water.

TEMPERATURE Maintain average temperatures. Keep temperatures in low 60s during bloom.

COMMENTS Train to circular wire or trellis. Vine curls up and around, overlapping earlier growth. Feed every 14 days with mild solution from spring to fall. Prune in spring, applying ash to cuts to stop bleeding. Propagate by cuttings taken in spring. Provide cuttings with lots of humidity and temperatures above 77 degrees.

MAIDENHAIR FERN

Adiantum (a-dee-AN-tum) species
Delta maidenhair, five-finger fern, southern maidenhair, venus's-hair

With thin, wiry stems and feathery fronds, maidenhair fern appears delicate, but it's really quite durable. Its fronds once were common in bouquets.

LIGHT Expose to medium (bright indirect) light. Tolerates low light. Keep out of full sun.

WATER Allow soil surface to dry out between thorough waterings. Never allow soil around roots to dry out. Mist daily with tepid water. Raise humidity as high as possible.

TEMPERATURE Maintain temperatures of no higher than low 70s during the day and into 50s at night for best growth. Tolerates average temperatures. Avoid hot and cold drafts.

COMMENTS Use soil rich in organic matter that retains moisture but drains freely. Feed every 21 days with super-mild solution. Do not overfertilize. Prune back to control size or stimulate new growth. Avoid the use of insecticides, which may kill the plant. Propagate by spores when fully formed or by division of mature plant in March.

Maidenhair fern

Mammillaria

Milkbush

MAMMILLARIA (mam-uh-LAIR-ee-uh)

Mammillaria species
Bird's-nest cactus, golden-star cactus, old-lady cactus, pincushion cactus, snowball cactus

Mammillaria cacti can be round- or cylinder-shaped, and soft- or sharp-spined. Choose several of the many species to form a fascinating plant collection that requires minimal attention. These cacti sometimes flower in early spring in colors that vary by species.

LIGHT Place in high light (southern exposure) year-round. Augment low light in winter with artificial light for 16 hours per day.

WATER Allow soil surface to dry out between thorough waterings. Water even less in winter, offering just enough to keep plant from withering.

TEMPERATURE Maintain average temperatures except during dormancy in winter. Then, let temperatures drop slightly.

COMMENTS Use a sandy medium. Feeding is unnecessary. Propagate by seed or offsets.

MILKBUSH

Euphorbia tirucalli
(you-FOR-bee-uh ter-uh-CAL-ee)
Pencil tree

Milkbush, which can grow as tall as 5 feet, has an unusual and highly sculptural look. The fleshy stems exude a milky, poisonous sap that can irritate the skin. Keep away from children.

LIGHT Place in high light in winter and medium (bright) light the rest of the year.

WATER Allow soil surface to dry out between thorough waterings. Water less during late fall and winter. Too much water causes root rot.

TEMPERATURE Maintain average temperatures. Tolerates from 50 to 80 degrees. Avoid cold drafts or frosty windowpanes.

COMMENTS Use porous soil for good drainage. Feed every 14 days from spring to fall. Propagate by stem cuttings in spring. Allow cuttings to dry for several days before planting.

MING ARALIA (uh-RAIL-ee-uh)

Polyscias fruticosa (poh-LIS-ee-us froo-ti-KOH-suh)

Ming aralia's dense, but delicate, foliage is dramatic against a white wall. The plant matures slowly and remains decorative for years.

LIGHT Expose to medium (indirect) light. Plant tolerates full sun several hours a day.

WATER Keep moist at all times. Water less during winter. Mist daily. Raise humidity.

TEMPERATURE Maintain temperatures between high 70s and low 80s, if possible. Tolerates average temperatures. Never let temperatures drop below 62 degrees at night. Avoid drafts.

COMMENTS Use a container appropriate for plant's size. Feed every 14 days during active growth with mild solution. Feed less in winter. Clean leaves monthly with warm water. Propagate by root division, stem cuttings, or air layering.

MONKEY-PUZZLE

Araucaria araucana
(ar-ah-KAIR-ee-uh ar-ah-KAIN-uh)

Monkey-puzzle is a slow-growing and unusual tree with shiny leaves and spiny branches. According to plant-name lore, monkey-puzzle gets its name from the fact that its upward-angled spines make it easy for monkeys to climb up the tree, but difficult for them to climb back down.

LIGHT Expose to medium (bright indirect) light. Avoid full sun. Set plant outside in summer in partial shade.

WATER Let soil surface dry out between thorough waterings. Water less in fall and winter, but do not let soil dry out completely.

TEMPERATURE Maintain average temperatures for best growth, although plant will tolerate much lower.

COMMENTS Plant in a deep pot, using a porous soil that drains freely. Feed monthly with dilute solution during active growth. Propagate by cutting off a growing tip, letting new growth emerge on the plant, then cutting and rooting the new growth. Provide cutting with lots of humidity.

Ming aralia

Monkey-puzzle

Moses-in-a-boat

MOSES-IN-A-BOAT

Rhoeo spathacea (REE-oh spay-THAY-see-uh)

Moses-in-a-boat's swordlike leaves are tinged purple underneath and support spathes (blooms) at the axils (where leaves and stem meet). The plant's name comes from the resemblance the axils and spathes have to boats with tiny white bundles. The plant, though, is grown mainly for its foliage.

LIGHT Expose to medium (bright indirect) light. Place outside in summer in the partial shade of an overhang.

WATER Keep evenly moist at all times, but avoid sogginess, which causes rot. Mist often. To keep leaves from rolling up, raise humidity.

TEMPERATURE Maintain high temperatures (to low 80s) for best growth. Plant tolerates average temperatures.

COMMENTS Grow one plant per pot for best effect. Pot up when partially root-bound. During active growth, feed every 14 days with mild solution. Rinse foliage monthly. Propagate by offsets or by the seedlings that often sprout up around plants in ideal settings, like greenhouses.

Moth orchid (left and above)

MOTH ORCHID

Phalaenopsis (fal-uh-NOP-sis) species

Moth orchid, which produces lovely, usually white blossoms on long stems, is one of the easiest orchids to get to rebloom each year. Its waxy blooms often are used in bridal bouquets. Varieties are available that bloom in colors other than white.

LIGHT Expose to medium (bright indirect) light. East window is best. Avoid full sun. Summer plant outside in partial shade.

WATER Keep evenly moist at all times. Mist daily. Raise humidity by setting pot on tray with moist pebbles. Outside, spray with fine mist daily.

TEMPERATURE Maintain high temperatures during the day for best growth. Plant tolerates average temperatures. Avoid cold drafts; keep away from windowpanes during winter.

COMMENTS Use orchid potting mix. Add mix each year after bloom. During active growth, feed every 14 days with a mild solution that has a high nitrogen content. To encourage reblooming, cut off flower stalks after final bloom. Propagate by crown division when several plants form at the base of the plant.

NERVE PLANT

Fittonia verschaffeltii
(fi-TOH-nee-uh vair-shaf-FEL-tee-eye)
Mosaic plant, red-nerve plant, silver-nerve

Fast growing and durable, nerve plant has attractive, intricately veined leaves. The leaf color varies by variety.

LIGHT Expose to medium (bright indirect) light. Avoid full sun. Grows well if under artificial light 14 hours per day.

WATER Allow soil to dry out between thorough waterings. Tolerates drought, but prefers misting and high humidity.

TEMPERATURE Maintain average temperatures. Never let temperature fall below 60 degrees.

COMMENTS Plant in shallow pot or hanging basket. Feed every 14 days with mild acid fertilizer. Remove any dry leaves. Pinch back to keep compact. To promote growth, pinch off any flower buds. Propagate by tip cuttings taken in spring.

Nerve plant

NORFOLK ISLAND PINE

Araucaria heterophylla
(ar-ah:KAIR-ee-uh het-er-oh-FIL-uh)

Graceful and well shaped, Norfolk Island pine has the delicately opposed branches of a pine tree. Needles are stiff, but soft. The tree grows slowly, producing one tier of opposed branches each year.

LIGHT Expose to medium (bright indirect) light. Avoid full sun. Sheds needles in low light. Place outdoors in shade during summer.

WATER Allow soil surface to dry between thorough waterings. Mist around but not directly on foliage. Likes humidity, but tolerates dryness.

TEMPERATURE Maintain cool temperatures (even into 40s) at night for best growth. Plant tolerates average temperatures. Avoid cold drafts.

COMMENTS Match pot size to plant. Use porous soil. Pot up into a pot two sizes larger when necessary. During active growth, feed every 21 days; reduce feeding in fall and winter. Propagate by seed or tip cutting. Cutting needs high humidity to root. Removal of tip will deform plant.

Norfolk Island pine

ORNAMENTAL PEPPER

Capsicum annuum (KAP-si-kum AN-new-um)

Pepper plants bear pretty blooms that develop into colorful fruits, many of which are edible as well as ornamental. Plants usually last only a year.

LIGHT Place in high light (southern exposure) indoors. Place outside in full sun in summer.

WATER Keep soil evenly moist. Mist daily. Raise humidity.

TEMPERATURE Maintain cool temperatures (at least in low 60s at night) for best growth. Tolerates average temperatures.

COMMENTS Plant in permanent pot from start. Feed only as needed for leaf color and fruit formation. Pinch or prune for desired shape. Remove fruit as needed. Propagate each year by seed.

OXALIS (ok-SAL-is)

Oxalis species
Irish shamrock, lucky clover, wood sorrel

Oxalis species come in many colors and leaf shapes. Fibrous-rooted types grow year-round; bulbous or semi-bulbous ones need rest after bloom.

LIGHT Place in high light in winter and medium (bright indirect) light rest of year. Vary location as necessary to provide just the right light.

WATER Keep evenly moist. Mist lightly each day. Avoid sogginess. Reduce water for bulbous and semi-bulbous varieties during dormancy. Increase water to stimulate new growth in spring.

TEMPERATURE Maintain average temperatures during day and cool temperatures (into 50s) at night. Keep bulbous and semi-bulbous varieties constantly cool (50 degrees) during dormancy.

COMMENTS Plant nine bulbs ½ inch deep in 5-inch pot. Avoid acid soil. Feed with dilute solution every 14 days March to late August. For bulbous and semi-bulbous types, reduce water and food to induce dormancy in fall and winter. Remove faded blossoms and spent foliage. Keep cool and barely moist. Water more in spring. Propagate by seed, root division, tip cuttings with a few varieties, or bulb offsets.

Ornamental pepper

Oxalis

Paper-white narcissus

PAPER-WHITE NARCISSUS (nar-SIS-us)

Narcissus tazetta (tuh-ZET-tuh)

One of the easiest bulbs to grow for scent, paper-white narcissus produces clusters of white blossoms atop tall, slender stems. It grows well in water (see right), or grow in soil as for other bulbs.

LIGHT Place in dark during root formation and high light during budding and flowering.

WATER Keep bulbs moist at all times. If allowed to dry, buds will fail to form or blooms will fade quickly.

TEMPERATURE Maintain cool temperatures for best growth. Tolerates average temperatures.

COMMENTS Fill shallow dish with pebbles or marble chips. Plant bulbs in dish so that half of each bulb is under the pebbles. Plant as many bulbs as the dish will allow without bulbs touching the side of the dish or each other. Moisten pebbles so that water just touches base of each bulb. Place dish in darkness for 10 days as roots form. Check moisture daily. When growth starts, bring bulbs gradually into bright light. Maintain temperatures in the low 60s. Place supports in dish to stop stems from toppling, or place rubber band around stems to keep them in a tight bunch. Discard bulbs after blooms fade. If you prefer to save bulbs, use soil culture as you would for crocus (see page 50), hyacinth (see pages 70–71), and other bulbs.

Parlor palm

Passionflower

PARLOR PALM

Chamaedorea elegans
(kam-ee-DOR-ee-uh EL-ee-ganz)
Good-luck palm

A slow-growing plant, parlor palm sprouts fronds up to 3 feet in length.

LIGHT Expose to medium (bright indirect) light year-round. Avoid full sun. Place outdoors in shade during summer. Tolerates low light. Grows well if under artificial light 16 hours per day.

WATER Allow soil surface to dry out between thorough waterings. Mist daily, especially during hot weather. Raise humidity.

TEMPERATURE Maintain high temperatures for best growth. Tolerates average temperatures. Avoid cold drafts.

COMMENTS Plant in deep pot. Use porous soil that drains freely. Feed monthly with very diluted mixture during active growth. Clean leaves monthly. Propagate by suckers or seed.

PASSIONFLOWER

Passiflora (pass-uh-FLOH-ruh) species
Granadilla

A fast-growing vine, passionflower boasts intricate and lovely flowers that last just a day. Some varieties are fragrant.

LIGHT Place in high light (southern exposure) during winter and medium (bright indirect) light the rest of the year.

WATER Keep soil evenly moist during active growth. Never let it dry out. Water less September through December. Mist daily. Raise humidity.

TEMPERATURE Maintain cool temperatures (into the 50s at night) for best growth. Tolerates average temperatures.

COMMENTS Plant in large container. Provide support. Feed weekly with dilute solution April through September. Prune to 8 inches each January. Pinch back to create side growth. Flowers grow only on new growth. Drip melted wax on base of petals to keep picked flowers open. Propagate by ground layering, stem cuttings, or seed.

Peacock plant

PEACOCK PLANT

Calathea makoyana
(kal-uh-THEE-uh mak-oh-YAY-nuh)
Brain plant, cathedral-windows

Peacock plant gets its name from the patterns on its leaves. More than 100 species of calathea exist, some of which are quite difficult to grow indoors.

LIGHT Place in high light year-round. Vary location by season for best results. Grows well if under artificial light 16 hours per day.

WATER Keep soil evenly moist during active growth. Water less during dormancy from October through February. Mist. High humidity essential.

TEMPERATURE Maintain high temperatures for best growth. Tolerates average temperatures.

COMMENTS Repot each year in June. Feed every 14 days during active growth. Clean leaves monthly. Avoid leaf polishes. Remove dead leaves. Pinch back if leggy or poorly shaped. Propagate by division, suckers, leaf cuttings, or seed (with some varieties) in spring.

Pellionia

PELLIONIA (pel-ee-OH-nee-uh)

Pellionia species
Rainbow vine, trailing watermelon begonia

Although slow growing, pellionia's trailing purple-tinged foliage makes it ideal for hanging displays. The plant is hard to find in some areas.

LIGHT Expose to medium (bright indirect) light. Plant tolerates low light. Grows well if under artificial light 14 hours per day.

WATER Keep very moist (almost wet), but avoid sogginess, which causes rot. Mist as often as possible. Raise humidity.

TEMPERATURE Maintain high temperatures for best growth. Tolerates average temperatures. Never let temperatures fall below 59 degrees.

COMMENTS Feed every 14 days with mild solution March through September. Prune back in spring if plant gets scruffy. Clean leaves every month. Propagate by tip cuttings.

PEPEROMIA (pep-uh-ROH-mee-uh)

Peperomia species
Numerous common names, most of them including the word peperomia

Peperomia is sold in a tremendous variety of forms, each with distinctive foliage. A few species produce flowers shaped similar to a rat's tail.

Peperomia (this page and opposite)

Persian-shield

LIGHT Expose to medium (bright indirect) light. Avoid full sun. Plant tolerates less light, but variegated species lose coloring in low light.

WATER Allow soil surface to dry between thorough waterings. Keep soil barely moist October through February. Avoid sogginess, which causes root rot. Mist. Raise humidity.

TEMPERATURE Maintain temperatures of 55 to 75 degrees.

COMMENTS Feed every 14 days with mild solution. Prune to maintain shape. Remove flowers in most varieties. Propagate by tip cuttings of vining varieties and leaf cuttings of nonvining types.

PERSIAN-SHIELD

Strobilanthes dyeranus
(stroh-bi-LAN-theez dy-er-AY-nus)

Persian-shield is grown as a foliage plant, although it can produce violet flowers on occasion.

LIGHT Expose to medium (bright indirect) light. Avoid full sun. Tolerates low light.

WATER Allow soil surface to dry out between thorough waterings. Do not let roots dry out.

TEMPERATURE Maintain temperatures of 55 to 70 degrees.

COMMENTS Feed lightly. Take tip cuttings.

PERSIAN VIOLET

Exacum affine (EKS-uh-kum af-FY-nee)
German violet

Persian violet produces pale blue, fragrant flowers in fall and winter. Start a new plant each year.

LIGHT Expose to medium (bright indirect) light. Plant does not bloom well in low light.

WATER Allow soil surface to dry between thorough waterings. Mist daily. Raise humidity.

TEMPERATURE Maintain temperatures of 60 to 70 degrees.

COMMENTS Feed every 14 days with mild solution during active growth. Remove spent blossoms. Propagate by seed, maintaining a soil temperature of 68 degrees or higher.

Persian violet

Philodendron (this page and opposite)

PHILODENDRON (fil-uh-DEN-drun)

Philodendron species
Numerous common names, most of them including the word philodendron

Whether erect or vining, philodendrons are among the most popular, easy, and durable of plants.

LIGHT Expose to medium (bright indirect) light. Avoid full sun. Tolerates low light. Proper light is the key to large leaves and rich color.

WATER Allow soil to dry out between thorough waterings. Mist frequently. Raise humidity.

TEMPERATURE Maintain temperatures in the 80s for best growth. Avoid all drafts.

COMMENTS Give support to vining varieties. Moisten support and aerial roots regularly. Feed every 14 days with mild solution. Sponge leaves clean with tepid water. Propagate by ground layering, stem cuttings, or seed (germination requires temperatures of 78 degrees or higher).

PIGGYBACK PLANT

Tolmiea menziesii (TOL-mee-uh men-ZEE-see-eye)
Pickaback plant, thousand-mothers, youth-on-age

Piggyback plant boasts pale green, fuzzy leaves that often support little plantlets piggyback-style. It looks best in hanging baskets.

LIGHT Expose to medium (bright indirect) light. Avoid full sun. Tolerates low light. Grows well if under artificial light 14 hours per day.

WATER Keep evenly moist at all times. Letting soil dry out will brown leaves and may kill plant. Mist daily. Raise humidity.

TEMPERATURE Maintain cool temperatures, especially in winter (mid-50s), for best growth. Tolerates average temperatures.

COMMENTS Feed every week with mild solution. Rinse foliage occasionally. Let drip-dry in low light. Propagate by division or by potting plantlets.

Piggyback plant

PLEOMELE (plee-OH-muh-lee)

Pleomele reflexa (ree-FLEKS-uh)
Song of India

Pleomele has narrow, leathery leaves that are edged with pale stripes in variegated varieties. It is dense and bushy, but can reach up to 12 feet in height. It's often called *Dracaena reflexa*.

LIGHT Expose to medium (bright indirect) light for best growth. Tolerates low light. Grows well if under artificial light 16 hours per day.

WATER Allow soil surface to dry out between thorough waterings. Never let soil dry out around roots. Mist frequently. Raise humidity.

TEMPERATURE Maintain temperatures in the 80s during the day for best growth. Tolerates average temperatures. Avoid cold drafts.

COMMENTS Use heavy, deep pot. Plant in porous soil. Pot up only when severely root-bound. Feed every 14 days with mild solution during active growth. Clean foliage monthly. Remove dead or dry leaves. When plant gets leggy and outgrows space, start new plant. Propagate by tip cuttings rooted in water or moist rooting medium.

Pleomele

POCKETBOOK FLOWER

Calceolaria herbeohybrida
(kal-see-uh-LAIR-ee-uh her-bee-oh-HIB-ri-duh)
Slipper flower

With its brightly colored and unusually shaped blooms, pocketbook flower is one of the most stunning gift plants.

LIGHT Place in medium (bright) light. Avoid full sun, which causes leaf burn.

WATER Allow soil surface to dry out between thorough waterings. Never allow soil around roots to dry out. Because blossoms spot easily, avoid getting water on them.

TEMPERATURE Maintain temperatures of 55 to 65 degrees, if possible. Tolerates average temperatures. Cool temperatures can extend bloom.

COMMENTS Discard most types after bloom (some shrub species can be carried over from year to year). Start fresh with seed each spring. Feed while young, but stop during bloom. Pinch during initial growth to create bushy plant.

PODOCARPUS (poh-doh-KAR-pus)

Podocarpus macrophyllus (mak-roh-FIL-us)
Buddhist pine, Japanese yew, southern yew

Sometimes used for bonsai, podocarpus has an airy, feathery look. Leaves get quite large—up to 4 inches long—and deep green with age. Place against a plain wall for a bold, architectural effect.

LIGHT Place in high light (southern exposure) during winter and medium (bright indirect) light the rest of the year. Tolerates low light.

WATER Allow soil surface to dry out between thorough waterings. Water less in fall and winter. Mist daily.

TEMPERATURE Maintain cool temperatures (to 40s at night) for best growth. Tolerates average temperatures.

COMMENTS Plant in tub. Use porous soil that drains freely. Feed every 14 days with dilute solution April through August. If desired, prune to keep small. Propagate by seed or cuttings from nearly ripe (not old, hard) wood.

Pocketbook flower

Podocarpus

POINSETTIA (poin-SET-ee-uh)

Euphorbia pulcherrima
(you-FOR-bee-uh pul-KER-ri-muh)

Poinsettia's bright pink, red, or white colors match the festive nature of the holiday season, and have made it one of the most popular gift plants in history. Unfortunately, poinsettias require special care to bring into bloom each year.

LIGHT Place in high light (southern exposure) when in flower, darkness for a time after bloom, then medium light when growing foliage. Strictly control light conditions in fall (see below).

WATER Allow soil surface to dry out between thorough waterings in spring and summer. Water less during fall and winter. Mist frequently and raise humidity during active growth.

TEMPERATURE Maintain average temperatures during day and cool temperatures (low 50s) at night, except after flowering, when cooler temperatures are needed. Avoid all drafts.

COMMENTS Water less and place in cool (no less than 45 degrees), dark place after flowering, when plant looks ragged. In spring, cut plant to height of 8 inches, leaving three nodes (where branches join stem) on each stem. On older plants, trim weak stems, leaving three to seven strong ones. Place outside in bright indirect light after frost danger passes. Keep moist. When growth starts, feed regularly. Pinch branches for bushiness, leaving four leaves on each. Bring in before frost. From October 1 to November 30, place plant in closet or bag from 5 p.m. to 8 a.m. This darkness is the key to getting red flowers (bracts) by Christmas. Repeat yearly. Propagate by tip cuttings.

Polka-dot plant

POLKA-DOT PLANT

Hypoestes phyllostachya
(hy-poh-EST-eez fil-oh-STAK-yuh)
Freckle-face, pink polka-dot plant

Pink- or rose-spattered leaves give polka-dot plant its appeal. It's sometimes sold as *H. sanguinolenta*.

LIGHT Place in high light in winter, medium light otherwise. Proper light is key to good color.

WATER Keep soil evenly moist during active growth. Water less in fall and winter. Mist daily. Raise humidity.

TEMPERATURE Maintain average temperatures. Plant tolerates higher and lower temperatures, but never set thermostat below 55 degrees.

COMMENTS Feed acid fertilizer every 14 days during active growth. Pinch back. Leaves may drop in fall and winter; water less and stop feeding at this time. Propagate by tip cuttings or seed.

Poinsettia (opposite and above)

Ponytail

Portulacaria

PONYTAIL

Beaucarnea recurvata
(boh-KAR-nee-uh reh-kur-VAY-tuh)
Bottle palm, elephant-foot tree

Ponytail stores water at its base, giving the plant's bottom its distinctive swollen look. Expect extremely slow growth, as little as 1 inch a year.

LIGHT Expose to medium (bright indirect) light. Avoid full sun. Tolerates low light. Grows well if under artificial light 14 hours per day.

WATER Allow soil to dry between thorough waterings. Plant tolerates drought when older. But don't let roots dry out completely. Mist frequently. Raise humidity.

TEMPERATURE Maintain average temperatures in the day. Keep temperatures in the middle 50s at night for best growth. Avoid drafts or frosty windows.

COMMENTS Feed every 14 days with dilute solution in spring and summer. In fall, reduce feeding, then stop in winter. Resume feeding in spring. Clean foliage monthly with tepid water. Propagate by offshoots or seed.

PORTULACARIA
(porch-uh-luh-KAIR-ee-uh)

Portulacaria afra (AY-fra)
Elephant bush, rainbow bush, and many other names depending on variety

A succulent shrub, elephant bush is reminiscent of jade plant, with smaller leaves and more angular growth. Use as a piece of living sculpture. The plant may flower indoors under ideal conditions, usually in a delicate pink or white.

LIGHT Place in high light during winter and in medium (bright indirect) light rest of year.

WATER Allow soil to dry out between thorough waterings. Plant tolerates drought. In fact, it likes dryness. Do not mist.

TEMPERATURE Maintain temperatures in the 80s for best growth. Plant tolerates average temperatures.

COMMENTS Use one-third coarse sand in potting mixture, if you like. Feed monthly with dilute solution. Trim to desired shape. Propagate by tip cuttings taken at time of pruning.

Prayer plant

PRAYER PLANT

Maranta (muh-RAN-tuh) species
Rabbit's-foot, rabbit's-tracks, ten-commandments

Maranta is grown for its colorful foliage and unusual habit of folding up at night as if in prayer.

LIGHT Expose to medium (bright indirect) light. Plant tolerates low light. Proper light is the key to good coloration. Morning light (eastern exposure) is ideal.

WATER Allow soil surface to dry out between thorough waterings. Mist daily. Raise humidity.

TEMPERATURE Maintain high temperatures (in the 80s during the day) for best growth. Tolerates average temperatures.

COMMENTS Plant in soil with lots of organic matter. Feed every 14 days with mild solution during active growth. Plant may go dormant in fall or winter. Remove old growth after this time. Because some prayer plants have tuberous roots, propagation method varies by variety. Propagate by tip cuttings, air layering, division, or seed.

Purple-passion vine

PURPLE-PASSION VINE

Gynura (jy-NOO-ruh) species
Purple velvet plant, royal velvet plant, velvet plant

Purple-passion vine, with its velvety, purplish leaves, creates a soft, luscious effect.

LIGHT Place in high light (southern exposure) during winter and medium (bright indirect) light the rest of the year. Grows well if under artificial light 14 hours per day.

WATER Keep evenly moist at all times, but avoid sogginess, which causes rot. Do not let soil dry out. Reduce watering in fall and winter. Mist daily. If water spotting occurs, move plant into less light. Raise humidity.

TEMPERATURE Maintain average temperatures during the day. For best growth, keep temperatures in the 50s at night.

COMMENTS Repot at least every two years to refresh soil. Feed every 14 days with mild solution during active growth. Pinch back to create bushiness. Remove dead leaves at once. Remove flowers for better growth. Propagate by tip cuttings.

Rex Begonia (buh-GOH-nyuh)

Begonia x rex-cultorum (REKS-cul-TOR-um)

Colored patterns and metallic markings make rex begonia a most desirable indoor plant.

LIGHT Expose to medium (bright indirect) light except in fall and winter, when light should be reduced. Avoid full sun.

WATER Keep soil evenly moist except in fall and winter, when watering should be reduced. Do not mist foliage. Raise humidity.

TEMPERATURE Maintain average temperatures during active growth. Cool temperatures (not below 60) better in fall-winter dormancy.

COMMENTS Plant rhizomes in shallow pot. Use peat-rich soil. Once plant is growing, feed every 14 days with dilute solution. Swirl dusty leaves in warm water; let drip-dry in warm room in low light. When leaves die back in fall, reduce watering and stop fertilizing. Store in cool, dark spot until February. Then, water more and bring into light. Propagate by seed or leaf cuttings.

Rex begonia

RIEGER BEGONIA
(RY-ger buh-GOH-nyuh)

Begonia x hiemalis (he-MAY-lis)
Elatior begonia, winter-flowering begonia

Whether trailing or upright, rieger begonia has waxy, dark green leaves and colorful flowers.

LIGHT Place in high light (southern exposure) in winter and medium (bright indirect) light rest of year. Summer outside in partial shade.

WATER Keep soil evenly moist except after bloom. Then, water less. Avoid splashing water on leaves, which may cause disease. Raise humidity.

TEMPERATURE Maintain temperatures in mid-50s to mid-60s. Average temperatures OK.

COMMENTS Feed monthly with dilute solution during active growth. Pinch in late spring and early summer for bushiness. Buds form in fall when days are short (10 hours of light). Keep out of light after dusk at this time. Blooms in six to nine weeks. Water less and stop feeding after bloom. When growth begins, water and feed normally.

Rieger begonia

ROSARY VINE
Ceropegia woodii
(seer-oh-PEE-gee-uh WOOD-ee-eye)
Hearts-entangled, hearts-on-a-string, heart vine, string-of-hearts

Rosary vine's heart-shaped leaves boast greenish silver on top and purple underneath. The stems sometimes carry light purple or pink flowers and little paired bulblets, resembling a rosary.

LIGHT Place in high light (southern exposure) in winter and medium (bright indirect) light the rest of the year.

WATER Allow soil to dry out between thorough waterings. Mist lightly.

TEMPERATURE Maintain average temperatures. Prefers cool temperatures (low 50s) at night.

COMMENTS Feed every 14 days with mild solution. Prune to base if plant looks rough. Propagate by rooting tip cuttings or by dividing and potting the little bulblets at base of plant and along the axils (where leaves and stem meet).

Rosary vine

Rubber plant

RUBBER PLANT

Ficus elastica (FY-kus ee-LAS-ti-kuh)

Durable and easy to care for, rubber plant is a bold tree that sports large, rubbery leaves on stems straight as exclamation points. Numerous varieties with slightly varied coloration exist. Expect lower leaves to drop over time.

LIGHT Expose to medium (bright indirect) light for best growth. Tolerates low light. Grows well if under artificial light 16 hours per day.

WATER Allow soil to dry out between thorough waterings. Mist frequently. Raise humidity.

TEMPERATURE Maintain high temperatures for best growth. Tolerates average temperatures.

COMMENTS Pot up only when severely rootbound. Use porous soil that drains freely. Pinch growing tip from young plant for multiple stem growth. Remove original leaf from immature, store-bought plant if it yellows, which is common. Feed every 14 days with mild solution during active growth. Clean leaves monthly. Avoid leaf polishes. Do not remove pink covering from newly forming leaf. Cut stem back to base if plant gets too large or leggy; stump will regenerate. Root tip for an additional plant. Propagate by air layering, tip cuttings, or leaf-bud cuttings.

Sago palm

Schefflera

SAGO PALM (SAY-go)

Cycas revoluta (SY-kus rev-oh-LOO-tuh)

Sago palm, despite its name, is not really a palm. Its trunk resembles a pinecone supporting fernlike fronds up to 5 feet long. The plant grows slowly, but can outgrow its space over a period of years.

LIGHT Place in medium light (eastern exposure) year-round. If placed outdoors in summer, locate in northern exposure.

WATER Keep evenly moist at all times. Water less during winter. Never let roots dry out.

TEMPERATURE Maintain average temperatures. Tolerates dips into the low 50s.

COMMENTS Pot up only when severely root-bound. Remove yellow fronds. Wash dust from fronds every three weeks. Many pesticides kill this plant, so read labels carefully. Because leaves bruise easily, place out of traffic. Propagate by seed or suckers in spring.

SCHEFFLERA (SHEF-luh-ruh)

Brassaia actinophylla
(BRASS-ee-uh ak-ti-noh-FIL-uh)
Umbrella tree

Schefflera forms canopies of branches that resemble small, glossy umbrellas. The plant blooms, but rarely indoors.

LIGHT Expose to medium (bright indirect) light. Avoid full sun. Low light produces sparse foliage. Grows well if under artificial light 16 hours per day.

WATER Allow soil to dry out between thorough waterings. Mist daily. Raise humidity.

TEMPERATURE Maintain high temperatures during the day for best growth. Tolerates average temperatures.

COMMENTS Feed every 14 days with mild solution during active growth. Clean leaves monthly with tepid water. Avoid leaf polishes. Pinch off growing tips to encourage side branching. Propagate by air layering, tip cuttings, or seed.

Screw pine

SCREW PINE

Pandanus (pan-DAY-nus) species

Tough and long-lived, screw pine looks like a trunkless palm. The leaves of some species have sawtooth edges. A native of Malaysia, screw pine, despite its name, is not part of the pine family.

LIGHT Expose to medium (bright indirect) light. Avoid full sun. Vary location by season for best results. Grows well if under artificial light 16 hours per day. Proper light is the key to maintaining variegation in some species.

WATER Allow soil to dry out between thorough waterings. Mist daily. Raise humidity, especially in the winter.

TEMPERATURE Maintain high temperatures for best growth. Tolerates average temperatures.

COMMENTS Pot in 10-inch clay pot, using porous soil that drains freely. Pot up only if severely root-bound. Guide aerial roots into soil; they'll take root. Feed every 14 days with mild solution during active growth. Clean leaves by running sponge up from base of plant. Remove dead leaves. Never use leaf polishes. Propagate by suckers.

SHRIMP PLANT

Justicia brandegeana
(jus-TIS-ee-uh bran-duh-juh-AY-nuh)

Shrimp plant shows off unusual blossoms (bracts) that resemble pale pink or yellow shrimp. It's often sold under its old name, *Beloperone guttata.*

LIGHT Place in high light (southern exposure) in winter and medium (bright indirect) light rest of year. Summer outside in partial shade.

WATER Allow soil surface to dry between thorough waterings. Water less in fall. Mist daily. Raise humidity.

TEMPERATURE Maintain temperatures to low 50s at night for best growth. Tolerates average temperatures. Keep cool during dormancy. Avoid cold or frost.

COMMENTS Pot up each February. Feed every 14 days with mild solution during active growth. Remove buds from young plants. Each fall, pinch back, reduce watering, and stop feeding; expect leaf drop. Propagate by tip cuttings of half-ripened (new, but firm) wood taken in April.

SNAKE PLANT

Sansevieria trifasciata
(san-suh-VEER-ee-uh try-fash-ee-AY-tuh)
Mother-in-law's-tongue

Snake plant—a strong vertical accent plant that comes in many varieties—is durable and easy to grow. Flowers indoors are rare, but memorable.

LIGHT Place in high light in winter and medium (bright indirect) light the rest of the year. Tolerates low light.

WATER Allow soil to dry between thorough waterings. Tolerates dry conditions well.

TEMPERATURE Maintain temperatures into the 80s during the day for best growth. Tolerates average temperatures.

COMMENTS Plant in shallow, heavy pot, using porous soil. Feed every week with mild solution. Clean leaves monthly. Remove dry leaves. Propagate by rhizome division, leaf cuttings, or offsets at base of plant.

Shrimp plant

Snake plant

Spathiphyllum

SPATHIPHYLLUM (spath-i-FIL-um)

Spathiphyllum species
Peace lily, spathe flower

Resembling calla lily, peace lily has long arching leaves and produces a spike of tiny yellow blossoms surrounded by a white spathe (flower).

LIGHT Expose to medium (bright indirect) light. Do not place in full sun. Tolerates low light, but normally needs brighter light to bloom.

WATER Keep soil evenly moist at all times. If soil dries out, the tips of leaves turn brown. Mist often. The higher the humidity, the better.

TEMPERATURE Maintain temperatures in the 80s during the day for best growth. Plant tolerates average temperatures.

COMMENTS Pot up each spring. If roots pop to soil surface, cover with sphagnum moss. From February through July, feed every 14 days with dilute solution. Remove yellow leaves. Propagate by seed anytime, or by dividing and potting the young shoots at the base of the plant in spring.

Spider plant

Staghorn fern

SPIDER PLANT

Chlorophytum comosum
(klor-oh-FY-tum koh-MOH-sum)
Airplane plant, ribbon plant, spider ivy

Spider plant may well be the easiest plant to grow indoors. The parent plant produces wiry stems covered with little plantlets that dangle in the air, mimicking a daddy longlegs spider.

LIGHT Expose to medium (bright indirect) light. Tolerates low light. Avoid full sun. Grows well if under artificial light 14 hours per day.

WATER Allow soil surface to dry out between thorough waterings. Mist frequently.

TEMPERATURE Maintain temperatures of 60 to 75 degrees.

COMMENTS Use soil mixes without perlite. Plant grows in water. Looks best in hanging basket. During active growth, feed weekly with mild solution. Propagate by dividing fleshy roots when they're mature or by potting the plantlets that form on the aerial runners.

STAGHORN FERN

Platycerium bifurcatum
(plat-i-SEER-ee-um by-fur-KAY-tum)

A true conversation piece, staghorn fern produces antlerlike fronds and grows rapidly to enormous size under ideal conditions.

LIGHT Expose to medium (bright indirect) light. Avoid full sun. East exposure is always best.

WATER Immerse base of plant twice a month into bath of warm water and dilute fertilizer. Never allow moss to dry out completely. Mist frequently. The higher the humidity, the better.

TEMPERATURE Maintain average temperatures. Avoid drafts.

COMMENTS Wrap base in peat and sphagnum moss, attach to a piece of cork or board with cotton fabric, then fasten board to wall. Or grow in hanging basket with sphagnum moss. Do not remove brown fronds at plant base. Avoid pesticides, which kill this plant. Plant forms plantlets at its base. Propagate by these plantlets or by spores.

Starfish flower

STARFISH FLOWER

Stapelia (stuh-PEEL-ee-uh) species
Carrion flower, hairy toad plant, starfish plant, toad plant

Truly one of the most bizarre houseplants, starfish flower produces a bloom that resembles the aquatic animal of its name. Some species emit an unpleasant odor that attracts pollinating flies.

LIGHT Place in high light (southern exposure) during winter and medium (bright indirect) light the rest of the year.

WATER Keep soil evenly moist, mist plant, and raise humidity in warm months. In cooler months, keep soil and air dry, and don't mist plant.

TEMPERATURE Maintain average temperatures. Plant tolerates temperatures as low as 50 degrees in winter. Avoid placing plant near frosty window or behind drawn curtain. Avoid drafts.

COMMENTS Pot up as necessary. Use humus-rich soil. Propagate by cuttings (most reliable to use whole leaf), division, or seed, depending on species. Dry cuttings before planting.

STRAWBERRY BEGONIA
(buh-GOH-nyuh)

Saxifraga stolonifera
(saks-IF-ruh-guh stoh-luh-NIF-er-uh)
Mother-of-thousands, strawberry geranium

Ideal for hanging displays, strawberry begonia is a low-growing trailer that produces round, hairy leaves and a profusion of little plantlets.

LIGHT Place in high light (southern exposure) during winter and medium (bright indirect) light the rest of the year.

WATER Allow soil surface to dry out between thorough waterings. Keep roots moist.

TEMPERATURE Maintain cool temperatures (even to low 40s) at night, if possible. Plant, however, tolerates average temperatures.

COMMENTS Feed every 14 days with mild solution March through September. Remove faded foliage or blossoms at once. Propagate by division or seed, or by potting plantlets on aerial runners.

Strawberry begonia

STREPTOCARPUS (strep-toh-KAR-pus)

Streptocarpus species
Cape primrose

Streptocarpus sends up flower-covered stems from the centers of fleshy-leaved rosettes. Each plant produces dozens of flowers under ideal conditions. A biennial, streptocarpus usually performs best in its second year of growth.

LIGHT Place in high light (full sun) in mid-winter and medium (bright) light rest of year.

WATER Allow soil surface to dry out slightly between thorough waterings. Water less during winter rest period. Raise humidity by setting pot on tray filled with moist pebbles.

TEMPERATURE Maintain temperatures of 55 to 60 degrees, if possible. Tolerates average temperatures if kept constantly moist. Keep temperatures in low 50s during winter dormancy.

COMMENTS Use shallow pots since roots are short. Use a growing medium that is half peat. Feed every 14 days during active growth. Because leaves break easily, place plant out of traffic. Plant goes through several months of dormancy each year after flowering. Cut back old growth at this time. Barely water and stop feeding. To break dormancy, start to water more freely. Water and feed normally once new growth emerges. Propagate by leaf cuttings (use wedges as with rex begonia), seed (start one year before expected bloom), or crown division (divide during dormancy).

Streptocarpus

STRING-OF-BEADS

Senecio rowleyanus
(si-NEE-shee-oh row-lee-AY-nus)

String-of-beads is a striking trailing plant with long stems resembling a string of pale green beads.

LIGHT Place in high light (southern exposure). Tolerates medium (bright) light.

WATER Allow soil to dry out between thorough waterings. Too much water causes rot.

TEMPERATURE Maintain average temperatures. Lower temperatures OK. Avoid drafts.

COMMENTS Use porous medium for good drainage. Feed yearly. Propagate by tip cuttings.

Swedish ivy

String-of-beads

SWEDISH IVY

Plectranthus (plek-TRAN-thus) species

A trailing plant that's not even an ivy, Swedish ivy produces long, squarish stems covered with scalloped, waxy leaves. It grows fast and is easy to take care of. Looks good in a hanging basket.

LIGHT Place in high light (southern exposure) during winter and medium (bright indirect) light rest of year. Tolerates low light. Grows well if under artificial light 14 hours per day.

WATER Allow soil surface to dry out between thorough waterings. Mist frequently.

TEMPERATURE Maintain average temperatures. Prefers temperatures into low 50s at night.

COMMENTS Feed every 14 days with mild solution from April through August. Pinch back ruthlessly to create a compact and bushy appearance. Propagate by seed in spring or tip cuttings anytime. Cuttings root easily in water.

Sweet potato

SWEET POTATO

Ipomoea batatas (ip-uh-MEE-uh buh-TAY-tus)
Sweet-potato vine, yam

Sweet potatoes, when placed in water or soil, produce extensive vines with attractive, heart-shaped leaves. The plants, which are fun projects for children, will last about a year in ideal conditions.

LIGHT Place in high light (southern exposure) at all times. Tolerates east and west light.

WATER Keep soil evenly moist at all times. Mist often. Raise humidity.

TEMPERATURE Maintain high temperatures for best growth. Tolerates average temperatures.

COMMENTS Start with firm potato. To grow in water, place three toothpicks equidistant around fat end of tuber. Rest on top of jar filled with water so that one-third of tuber is submerged. Add charcoal to water. Change water weekly. To grow in soil, plant potato on its side about 2 inches deep. In either medium, roots will sprout, as will growth from eyes of tuber. Train vine as desired. Pinch tips for bushiness. Plant rooted slips (tip cuttings) outside in spring for sweet potato crop.

Swiss-cheese plant

SWISS-CHEESE PLANT

Monstera deliciosa
(MON-ster-uh del-ish-ee-OH-suh)
Hurricane plant, Mexican breadfruit, split-leaf philodendron

Easy to grow and durable, Swiss-cheese plant boasts vining stems and broad, dark green leaves.

LIGHT Expose to medium (bright indirect) light. Tolerates low light, although the dimmer the light, the less the leaves develop their characteristic holes and slashes. Grows well if under artificial light 16 hours per day.

WATER Let soil surface dry out between thorough waterings. Mist frequently. Raise humidity.

TEMPERATURE Maintain temperatures in the 80s during the day, if possible. Tolerates average temperatures.

COMMENTS Plant in large pot with adequate support for vine. Feed every 14 days with mild solution during active growth. Clean leaves monthly. Avoid leaf polishes. Propagate by air layering, seed, leaf-bud cuttings, or tip cuttings.

TI PLANT (TEE)

Cordyline terminalis (kor-di-LY-nee ter-mi-NAL-is)
Good-luck plant, tree-of-kings

Sturdy ti plant shows off magnificent light pink and yellow leaves. Be patient since leaf coloration intensifies with age.

LIGHT Expose to medium (bright indirect) light. Move with the seasons for ideal location. Summer outside in partial shade or filtered light.

WATER Allow soil to dry out between thorough waterings. Mist daily. Raise humidity.

TEMPERATURE Maintain temperatures in the 80s during the day, if possible. Tolerates average temperatures.

COMMENTS Pot up only when severely rootbound. Feed every 14 days with a mild solution during active growth. Clean foliage with warm water. Avoid leaf polishes. Propagate by stem cuttings—the little "logs" sold as novelties in garden centers—or by air layering.

Ti plant

TREE IVY

Fatshedera lizei (fat-SED-uh-ruh LY-zee-eye)
Aralia ivy, botanical-wonder, ivy tree

Whether shrub or vine, tree ivy produces glossy, green, ivy-shaped leaves. It's especially effective when several plants are grown together and trained to a central stake, creating a high vertical column of foliage.

LIGHT Expose to medium (bright indirect) light for best growth. Tolerates low light. Place in partial shade or filtered light outdoors. Grows well if under artificial light 16 hours per day.

WATER Keep soil evenly moist. Dry soil can cause leaves to drop. Mist daily. Raise humidity.

TEMPERATURE Maintain temperatures from 60 to 70 degrees. Tolerates 50 to 80 degrees.

COMMENTS Feed monthly with dilute solution during active growth. Likes being pot-bound. Clean leaves monthly with warm water. Avoid leaf polishes. If placed outside, protect from wind to keep leaves from shredding. Prune to desired shrub form or support with stake. Propagate by stem cuttings or air layering.

117

Tuberous begonia

TUBEROUS BEGONIA
(TOO-ber-us buh-GOH-nyuh)

Begonia x tuberhybrida (too-ber-HIB-ri-duh)

Spectacular bloomers, tuberous begonias send up flowers in a variety of colors, sizes, and shapes.

LIGHT Expose to medium (bright indirect) light during active growth, dark during dormancy.

WATER Keep constantly moist during active growth. Water less after foliage starts to yellow, then stop during dormancy. Raise humidity.

TEMPERATURE Maintain average temperatures during active growth and cooler temperatures during dormancy.

COMMENTS Plant tubers, hollow side up and barely exposed, in shallow pots; use soil high in organic matter. Keep moist and at 70 degrees to spur growth. Water and feed regularly. After bloom, water less until leaves wilt. Clean and dry tubers; store in cool, dry, dark place. Or, leave in pot on side in similar spot. Propagate by cutting shoots (eyes) off tubers. Use as tip cuttings.

Tulip

Umbrella plant

TULIP

Tulipa (TOO-lip-uh) hybrids

Bought in bloom or as a bulb to be forced, tulip makes a stunning midwinter display.

LIGHT Place in dark while chilling, medium light during early growth, and high light during bloom and subsequent growth.

WATER Keep barely moist during chilling. Water more in early growth. Keep evenly moist during bud and flower, and until foliage dies back.

TEMPERATURE Keep at 50 degrees while chilling. Raise to low 60s during bud and bloom. Keep below 50 degrees till planting outside.

COMMENTS Place bulbs close together in pot; don't allow them to touch each other or pot sides. Cover with soil; moisten. Set in dark at 50 degrees until growth is 4 inches high (usually in 10 to 12 weeks). Bring into warmth and medium light. When buds form, place in high light. After bloom, water and feed until foliage dies down. Clean bulbs and store in cool spot. Plant outside in spring.

UMBRELLA PLANT

Cyperus alternifolius
(sy-PEER-us al-ter-ni-FOH-lee-us)
Umbrella palm, umbrella sedge

Shiny, narrow leaves form small umbrellas atop the slender grassy stems of umbrella plant. An aquatic plant, umbrella plant needs constant moisture. Dwarf varieties are easiest to grow. Do not confuse this plant with umbrella tree (schefflera).

LIGHT Place in high light (full sun) in winter and medium (bright indirect) light rest of year. Grows well if under artificial light 14 hours a day.

WATER Keep constantly wet by placing pot in water-filled saucer. Mist often. Raise humidity.

TEMPERATURE Maintain average temperatures. Plant prefers cool temperatures (to mid-50s) at night.

COMMENTS Feed every 14 days with dilute acid solution during active growth. If plant looks bad, cut back to base. Propagate by leaf-bud cuttings (start in water), division, suckers, or seed.

Venus's-flytrap

Vriesea

VENUS'S-FLYTRAP

Dionaea muscipula
(dy-oh-NEE-uh mus-KIP-you-luh)

Grown as a novelty, venus's-flytrap digests insects in traplike leaves. It does not need bugs to survive.

LIGHT   Place in high light (southern exposure) for best color. Tolerates low light in summer.

WATER   Keep evenly moist or wet. Mist daily. Raise humidity. Does not tolerate dryness.

TEMPERATURE   Maintain temperatures in the 40s at night and no higher than low 60s during the day. Barely tolerates average temperatures.

COMMENTS   Plant in shallow container filled with sphagnum moss. If you use soil, add peat moss. Do not fertilize. Do not feed plant insects during winter; may cause its death. Remove flowers when they appear because plant needs cross-pollination to form seed. Parent plants often die as offspring appear. Propagate by seed or division.

VRIESEA (VREE-zee-uh)

Vriesea species
Flaming-sword, lobster-claws, painted-feather

One of the showier bromeliads to grow indoors, vriesea forms a stunning vertical spike (bract) on a slender stalk.

LIGHT   Place in high light (southern exposure) during winter and medium (bright indirect) light rest of year. Tolerates low light.

WATER   Keep soil moist at all times. Avoid sogginess. Mist daily with tepid water. Keep humidity as high as possible.

TEMPERATURE   Maintain high temperatures (to 80s), if possible. Plant tolerates average temperatures. Avoid cold drafts.

COMMENTS   Use orchid potting mix. Drench growing medium and spray foliage with dilute fertilizer solution. Avoid insecticides. Stimulate flowering by placing plant in sealed plastic bag with ripening apple; ethylene given off by fruit encourages flowering. Propagate by separating young plants that grow to side or in center of old plant.

Waffle Plant

Hemigraphis (hem-i-GRAF-is) species
Purple waffle plant, red-flame ivy, red ivy

A creeper, waffle plant boasts deep green leaves with reddish undersides. It occasionally produces clusters of white flowers.

LIGHT Expose to medium (bright indirect) light. Plant changes color under varying conditions, from silvery in low light to reddish in sun. Grows well if under artificial light 14 hours a day.

WATER Keep soil evenly moist. Mist daily. Raise humidity.

TEMPERATURE Maintain average temperatures. Avoid cold drafts.

COMMENTS Grow as ground cover in large pot or in a hanging basket. Plant in soil with lots of organic matter. Feed monthly with a dilute solution during active growth. Pinch back ruthlessly for compact growth. Propagate by rooting tip cuttings or dividing plants where they take root.

Waffle plant

Wandering Jew

Tradescantia (trad-uh-SKAN-shee-uh) species or *Zebrina* (zi-BRY-nuh) species

No plant is easier to grow or better suited for a hanging basket than wandering Jew. Grown for its colorful foliage, the plant occasionally blooms.

LIGHT Place in high to medium (bright indirect) light, depending on desired coloration. Full sun may turn plants of some varieties pure green.

WATER Keep evenly moist. Mist daily. Raise humidity. Avoid sogginess, which causes root rot.

TEMPERATURE Maintain average temperatures. Tolerates high and low. Avoid cold drafts.

COMMENTS Place where branches can dangle freely. Use porous soil. Feed every 14 days with dilute solution during active growth. Do not overfeed; can cause leaves to pale. Stop feeding from fall to midwinter. Prune ruthlessly to encourage branching and maintain attractive shape. If colored foliage turns green, pinch off green growth and move into lower light. Wash foliage monthly. Propagate by tip cuttings.

Wandering Jew

Wax begonia

WAX BEGONIA (buh-GOH-nyuh)

Begonia x semperflorens-cultorum
(sem-per-FLOH-renz kul-TOR-um)
Bedding begonia

Often thought of as an outdoor bedding plant, wax begonia grows well indoors, too.

LIGHT Place in high light (full sun) for best growth. Tolerates medium (bright indirect) light.

WATER Allow soil surface to dry slightly between thorough waterings. Mist daily with tepid water. Raise humidity.

TEMPERATURE Maintain average temperatures during the day, but let them fall into the 50s at night. May not bloom in high temperatures.

COMMENTS Feed every few weeks with dilute solution during active growth. Pinch tips for bushiness. Propagate by seed or tip cuttings.

WAX PLANT

Hoya (HOY-uh) species
Hindu-rope, honey plant

Attractive for its foliage, wax plant rewards those willing to wait a few years with shiny, sweetly scented flowers.

LIGHT Place in high light (southern exposure) in late winter and medium (bright indirect) light rest of year. In summer, place outdoors in partial shade or filtered light.

WATER Keep soil evenly moist except during dormancy in the fall, when soil should be kept nearly dry. Mist with tepid water.

TEMPERATURE Maintain average temperatures during active growth and temperatures in the low 60s during dormancy.

COMMENTS Support vining varieties or grow in hanging baskets. Keep cool and nearly dry during dormancy in the fall. Pot up young plants in February. Provide warmth and moisture to initiate new growth. Feed monthly, less often when in bloom. Because flowers appear on old spurs, never prune this plant. Never move plant during budding. Propagate by tip cuttings taken in spring.

Wax plant

Weeping fig

WEEPING FIG

Ficus benjamina (FY-kus ben-juh-MY-nuh)

Weeping fig is one of the finest indoor trees. Its branches weep slightly and are covered with shiny, small leaves.

LIGHT Expose to medium (bright indirect) light. Place outdoors in filtered light during summer. Intense light pales foliage.

WATER Allow soil to dry out between thorough waterings. Mist frequently. Prefers higher humidity, but tolerates dry conditions.

TEMPERATURE Maintain average temperatures. Avoid cold drafts.

COMMENTS Pot up as needed; plant will get large. Feed every 14 days with mild solution during active growth. Prune to desired shape in spring. Expect some leaves to yellow and drop from weeping fig after any move and in winter. Propagate by air layering.

YUCCA (YUK-uh)

Yucca elephantipes (el-ee-FAN-ti-pus)
Spineless yucca

Spineless yucca is one of the more difficult indoor plants to grow, but it's well worth trying. The plant boasts rigid, tightly packed, swordlike leaves on a woody stem that may grow 6 feet tall or more. *Yucca aloifolia,* often called Spanish-bayonet, is shorter and sends up just one rosette of leaves.

LIGHT Place in high light (full sun) for best growth. Always place plant outdoors in summer.

WATER Let soil dry out between thorough waterings. Avoid soggy conditions. Tolerates low humidity. Misting not necessary.

TEMPERATURE Maintain average temperatures; tolerates a range of 55 to 80 degrees. Prefers a drop of 10 degrees at night.

COMMENTS Feed every three weeks with dilute solution during active growth, usually late spring through summer. Susceptible to leaf spot. Remove infected leaves immediately. Avoid leaf polishes. Propagate by root cuttings or offsets.

ZEBRA PLANT

Aphelandra squarrosa
(af-uh-LAN-druh skwah-ROH-suh)
Saffron-spike

Zebra plant forms a spike several inches high that may last up to six weeks in hot, humid conditions.

LIGHT Place in high light (south exposure) in winter, medium (bright indirect) light rest of year.

WATER Keep evenly moist. Water a little less during and just after bloom. Reduce in dormancy. Mist often. Raise humidity as high as possible.

TEMPERATURE Maintain high temperatures for best growth. Never let temperatures drop below 65 degrees.

COMMENTS Cut to 6 inches in March. Trim part of roots. Repot in same pot. Once growing well, feed every 14 days with full doses. Will reflower in fall. Allow to rest six weeks after last flower by reducing food and water. Propagate by seed anytime or stem cuttings taken at pruning.

Yucca

Zebra plant

INDEX

A–B

Abutilon species, 62
Acalypha hispida, 44
Achimenes species, 19, 27
Adiantum species, 84
Aechmea fasciata, 27
Aeschynanthus species, 82
African evergreen, 8, 31
African lily, 81
African violet, 16, 21, 22, 28
Agapanthus species, 81
Aglaonema species, 8, 44
Air layering, 20, 21–22
Airplane plant, 22, 111
Alligator pear, 33
Aloe vera, 28
Amaryllis, 29, 75
Amazon lily, 30
Angel's-tears, 34
Angel-wing begonia, 30
Anthurium species, 31
Aphelandra squarrosa, 124
Aphids, 23. *See also* Insects
Arabian coffee, 46
Aralia ivy, 117
Aralias, 34, 59, 86
Araucaria araucana, 86
Araucaria heterophylla, 16, 89
Areca palm, 40
Aristocrat plant, 68
Arrowhead vine, 8, 31
Artificial light, 11–12. *See also* Light
Asparagus fern, 18, 32
Aspidistra elatior, 43
Asplenium nidus, 37
Aucuba japonica, 32
Avocado, 33
Axils, defined, 5, 87, 105
Azalea, 9, 14, 15, 33
Baby's-tears, 34
Balfour aralia, 34
Bamboo palm, 35
Banana plant, 36
Bark, shredded, 9
Barroom plant, 43
Basket vine, 82
Beaucarnea recurvata, 102
Bedding begonia, 122
Begonia
  angel-wing, 30
  bedding, 122
  elatior, 105
  iron-cross, 73
  propagating, 21
  rex, 21, 104, 113
  rieger, 105
  strawberry, 22, 112
  trailing watermelon, 94
  tuberous, 19, 118
  wax, 122
  winter-flowering, 105
Begonia
  coccinea, 30
  masoniana, 73
  x *hiemalis*, 105
  x *rex-cultorum*, 21, 104, 113
  x *semperflorens-cultorum*, 122
  x *tuberhybrida*, 19, 118
Beloperone guttata, 109
Bird-of-paradise, 36–37
Bird's-nest cactus, 85
Bird's-nest fern, 37
Blood meal, 14
Bonemeal, 14
Bonsai, 99
Boston fern, 38
Botanical-wonder, 117
Bottle palm, 102
Bougainvillea species, 38
Bracts, defined, 51, 101, 109, 120
Brain plant, 93
Brake fern, 39
Brassaia actinophylla, 11, 22, 107, 119
Breadfruit, Mexican, 116
Bright indirect light, defined, 11
Bromeliads
  aechmea fasciata, 27
  cryptanthus species, 52
  earth-star, 52
  flaming-sword, 120
  guzmania lingulata, 68
  living-vase, 27
  lobster-claws, 120
  painted-feather, 120
  propagating, 18, 22
  soil, 9
  urn plant, 27
  vriesea species, 120
Buddhist pine, 99
Burn plant, 28
Burro's-tail, 39
Busy lizzy, 18, 72
Butterfly palm, 40

C–F

Cacti. *See* Succulents and cacti
Caladium species, 19, 40–41
Calamondin orange, 41
Calathea makoyana, 93
Calceolaria herbeohybrida, 99
Calla lily, 42, 110
Camellia species, 9, 15, 42–43
Cape jasmine, 15, 64
Cape primrose, 113
Capsicum annuum, 90
Carrion flower, 112
Caryota mitis, 60–61
Cast-iron plant, 43
Cathedral-windows, 93
Ceropegia woodii, 105
Chamaedorea elegans, 92
Chamaedorea erumpens, 35
Chamaerops humilis, 58
Charcoal, 8, 9
Chenille plant, 44
Children, and houseplants, 25
Chinese evergreen, 8, 44
Chinese hibiscus, 69
Chinese-lantern, 62
Chinese rose, 69
Chinese rubber plant, 74, 102
Chlorophytum comosum, 22, 111
Christmas cactus, 11, 14, 23, 45
Christmas kalanchoe, 11, 18, 76–77
Chrysalidocarpus lutescens, 40
Chrysanthemum, 11, 45
Cissus antarctica, 77
Cissus rhombifolia, 8, 67
Citrus limon, 80
Citrus mitis, 41
Cleaning
  houseplants, 16–17
  pots, 8
Climbing fig, 49
Clivia miniata, 75
Clover, lucky, 90
Codiaeum variegatum, 8, 11, 51
Coffea arabica, 46
Coleus species, 8, 16, 18, 46–47
Columnea species, 47
Compost, 9
Convallaria majalis, 81
Cordyline terminalis, 116
Corn plant, 48
Corsican carpet plant, 34
Corsican-curse, 34
Crassula argentea, 74, 102
Creeping charlie, 13, 49
Creeping fig, 49
Creeping rubber plant, 49
Crocus species, 50, 91
Crossandra infundibuliformis, 60
Croton, 8, 11, 51
Crown-of-thorns, 51
Cryptanthus species, 52
Cushion aloe, 68
Cuttings, 5, 19, 21
Cycas revoluta, 107
Cyclamen species, 19, 52
Cymbidium hybrids, 53
Cyperus alternifolius, 119
Cyrtomium falcatum, 70
Damping-off, 8, 18, 23
Decorating with houseplants, 25
Delta maidenhair, 84
Dendranthema grandiflora, 11, 45
Devil's-backbone, 53
Devil's ivy, 8, 21, 54
Dieffenbachia species, 8, 20, 21, 22, 54
Dionaea muscipula, 120
Diseases, 5, 23
Division, 19

Dizygotheca elegantissima, 59
Double potting, 14, 15, 23
Dracaena
   fragrans 'massangeana,' 48
   marginata, 55
   reflexa, 98
   propagating, 21, 22
   water, growing in, 8
Dragon tree, 55
Dumb cane, 8, 20, 21, 22, 54
Dwarf fan palm, 58
Earth-star, 52
Easter cactus, 45
Easter lily, 55
Easy-care houseplants, 25
Echeveria species, 56
Elatior begonia, 105
Elephant bush, 102
Elephant-foot tree, 102
English ivy, 8, 56–57, 65
Epipremnum aureum, 8, 21, 54
Episcia species, 22, 61
Eucharis grandiflora, 30
Euphorbia pulcherrima, 11,
   100–101
Euphorbia splendens, 51
Euphorbia tirucalli, 85
European fan palm, 58
Exacum affine, 96
False aralia, 59
Fancy-leaved caladium, 19, 40–41
Fatshedera lizei, 117
Feeding houseplants, 14–15
Ferns
   adiantum species, 84
   asparagus, 18, 32
   asplenium nidus, 37
   bird's-nest, 37
   Boston, 38
   brake, 39
   cleaning, 17
   cyrtomium falcatum, 70
   delta maidenhair, 84
   five-finger, 84
   holly, 70
   Japanese holly, 70
   lace, 18, 32
   maidenhair, 84
   nephrolepis exaltata
     'Bostoniensis,' 38
   platycerium bifurcatum, 111
   propagating, 19
   pteris species, 39
   southern maidenhair, 84
   staghorn, 111
   table, 39
   venus's-hair, 84
Fertilizers, 14–15
Ficus
   ficus benjamina, 17, 123
   ficus elastica, 106
   ficus lyrata, 59
   ficus pumila, 49
   propagating, 22
Fiddle-leaf fig, 59
Firecracker flower, 60
First-aid plant, 28

Fish emulsion, 8, 14
Fishtail palm, 60–61
Fittonia verschaffeltii, 89
Five-finger fern, 84
Flame nettle, 8, 16, 18, 46–47
Flame-of-the-woods, 73
Flame violet, 22, 61
Flamingo flower, 31
Flaming-sword, 120
Floradora, 83
Flowering maple, 62
Flowering-stones, 82
Freckle-face, 101
Freesia species, 63
Fuchsia x hybrida, 63
Full sun, defined, 11

G–L

Garden croton, 8, 11, 51
Gardenia jasminoides, 15, 64
Geranium, 16, 65
   jungle, 73
   strawberry, 112
German ivy, 65
German violet, 96
Gift houseplants, 24
Gloxinia, 18, 19, 21, 47, 66–67
Gold-dust plant, 32
Golden pothos, 8, 21, 54
Golden-star cactus, 85
Goldfish plant, 47
Good-luck palm, 92
Good-luck plant, 116
Granadilla, 92
Grape ivy, 8, 67
Ground layering, 22
Growing media, 8–9, 18
Guzmania lingulata, 68
Gynura species, 103
Hairy toad plant, 112
Hardening off, defined, 15
Haworthia species, 68
Hearts-entangled, 105
Hearts-on-a-string, 105
Heart vine, 105
Hedera helix, 8, 56–57, 65
Helxine soleirolii, 34
Hemigraphis species, 121
Hibiscus rosa-sinensis, 69
High light, defined, 11
Hindu-rope, 21, 122
Hippeastrum species, 29, 75
Holly fern, 70
Honey plant, 21, 122
Howea forsterana, 78, 79
Hoya species, 21, 122
Humidity, 14, 18, 23
Hurricane plant, 116
Hyacinthus orientalis, 70–71, 91
Hydrangea macrophylla, 71, 73
Hypoestes phyllostachya, 101
Hypoestes sanguinolenta, 101
Impatiens wallerana, 18, 72
Indian mallow, 62
Indirect light, defined, 11

Insects, 5, 14, 23
Ipomoea batatas, 8, 115
Irish moss, 34
Irish shamrock, 90
Iron-cross begonia, 73
Ivy tree, 117
Ixora species, 73
Jade plant, 74, 102
Japanese holly fern, 70
Japanese laurel, 32
Japanese moss, 34
Japanese yew, 99
Jardinieres, 7. *See also* Pots
Jerusalem cherry, 74
Joseph's coat, 8, 11, 51
Jungle-flame, 73
Jungle geranium, 73
Justicia brandegeana, 109
Kaffir lily, 75
Kalanchoe blossfeldiana, 11, 18,
   76–77
Kangaroo vine, 77
Kelp, 14, 15
Kentia palm, 78, 79
Lace fern, 18, 32
Ladies'-eardrops, 63
Lady palm, 78, 79
Lady's-slipper, 79
Lantana camara, 16, 80
Leaf-bud cuttings, 21
Leaf cuttings, 21
Leaf mold, 9
Lemon tree, 80
Light, 11–12, 15, 18, 19, 24
Lilium longiflorum, 55
Lily-of-the-Nile, 81
Lily-of-the-valley, 81
Lipstick plant, 82
Lithops species, 82
Living-stones, 82
Living-vase, 27
Loam, black, 9. *See also* Soil
Lobster-claws, 120
Low light, defined, 11
Lucky clover, 90

M–O

Madagascar dragon tree, 55
Madagascar jasmine, 83
Magic flower, 19, 27
Maidenhair fern, 84
Malathion, 23
Mammillaria species, 85
Manure, 9, 14
Maranta species, 103
Mealybugs, 5, 23. *See also* Insects
Medicinal aloe, 28
Medium light, defined, 11
Mexican breadfruit, 116
Milkbush, 85
Mimicry plant, 82
Mind-your-own-business, 34
Ming aralia, 86
Misting houseplants, 14, 18
Miticides, 23

Monkey-faced pansy, 19, 27
Monkey-puzzle, 86
Monstera deliciosa, 116
Mosaic plant, 89
Moses-in-a-boat, 87
Moss
  peat, 9, 18, 19, 21, 22
  sphagnum, 14, 18, 22
Mother-in-law plant, 8, 20, 21,
  22, 54
Mother-in-law's-tongue, 21, 109
Mother-of-thousands, 22, 112
Moth orchid, 88
Moving houseplants, 6, 23
Mum, 11, 45
Musa species, 36
Narcissus tazetta, 91
Nephrolepis exaltata
  'Bostoniensis,' 38
Nephthytis species, 8, 31
Nerve plant, 89
Nitrogen, 14
Nodes, defined, 16, 19, 21, 101
Norfolk Island pine, 16, 89
Norse fire plant, 47
Offsets, 22
Offshoots, 22
Old-lady cactus, 85
Orange, calamondin, 41
Orchid pansy, 19, 27
Orchids
  cymbidium hybrids, 53
  lady's-slipper, 79
  moth, 88
  paphiopedilum species, 79
  phalaenopsis species, 88
  slipper, 79
  soil, 9
Ornamental pepper, 90
Oxalis species, 90

P–R

Painted drop-tongue, 8, 44
Painted-feather, 120
Painted leaves, 8, 16, 18, 46–47
Painted nettle, 8, 16, 18, 46–47
Painter's palette, 31
Palms
  areca, 40
  bamboo, 35
  bottle, 102
  butterfly, 40
  caryota mitis, 60–61
  chamaedorea elegans, 92
  chamaedorea erumpens, 35
  chamaerops humilis, 58
  chrysalidocarpus lutescens, 40
  cycas revoluta, 107
  dwarf fan, 58
  European fan, 58
  fishtail, 60–61
  good-luck, 92
  howea forsterana, 78, 79
  kentia, 78, 79
  lady, 78, 79

Palms *(continued)*
  parlor, 92
  propagating, 22
  pruning, 16
  rhapis species, 78, 79
  sago, 107
  slender lady, 78, 79
  umbrella, 119
Pandanus species, 22, 108
Paper flower, 38
Paper-white narcissus, 91
Paphiopedilum species, 79
Parlor ivy, 65
Parlor maple, 62
Parlor palm, 92
Passiflora, 92
Passionflower, 92
Patience plant, 18, 72
Patient lucy, 18, 72
Peace lily, 110
Peacock plant, 93
Pearl plant, 68
Peat moss, 9, 18, 19, 21, 22
Pebbles, uses of, 14, 15, 23
Pedilanthus tithymaloides, 53
Pelargonium species, 16, 65
Pellionia species, 94
Pencil tree, 85
Peperomia species, 11, 94–95
Pepper, ornamental, 90
Perlite, 9, 18, 19, 21
Persea americana, 33
Persian-shield, 95
Persian violet, 96
Phalaenopsis species, 88
Philippine-medusa, 44
Philodendron, split-leaf, 116
Philodendron species, 8, 21, 96–97
Phosphorus, 14
Pickaback plant, 22, 98
Piggyback plant, 22, 98
Pigtail plant, 31
Pilea nummulariifolia, 13, 49
Pincushion cactus, 85
Pink polka-dot plant, 101
Pips, defined, 81
Platycerium bifurcatum, 111
Plectranthus species, 8, 114–115
Pleomele reflexa, 98
Pocketbook flower, 99
Podocarpus macrophyllus, 99
Poinsettia, 11, 100–101
Polka-dot plant, 101
Polyscias balfouriana, 34
Polyscias fruticosa, 86
Ponytail, 102
Poor man's orchid, 19, 52
Portulacaria afra, 102
Potassium, 14
Pothos, 8, 21, 54
Pots, 7, 8, 10, 13, 15
Potting on. *See* Potting up
Potting soil, 9, 18
Potting up, 10, 19, 21
Prayer plant, 103
Primrose, cape, 113
Propagation, 5, 18–22

Pruning houseplants, 16, 17
Pteris species, 39
Purple-passion vine, 103
Purple velvet plant, 103
Purple waffle plant, 121
Pyrethrum, 23
Rabbit's-foot, 103
Rabbit's-tracks, 103
Rainbow bush, 102
Rainbow vine, 94
Red-flame ivy, 121
Red-hot cattail, 44
Red ivy, 121
Red-nerve plant, 89
Red spider mites, 5, 14, 23
Repotting, 10. *See also* Pots
Rex begonia, 21, 104, 113
Rhapis species, 78, 79
Rhododendron species, 9, 14,
  15, 33
Rhoeo spathacea, 87
Ribbon plant, 22, 111
Rieger begonia, 105
Root-bound, 7, 10
Root cuttings, 21
Rooting hormone powder, 19, 20,
  21, 22
Rooting media, 19–20
Root rot, 7, 12, 13, 14. *See also*
  Stem rot
Rosary vine, 105
Rot
  root, 7, 12, 13, 14
  stem, 23
Royal velvet plant, 103
Rubber plant, 106
Runners, 22

S

Saffron-spike, 124
Sage, yellow, 16, 80
Sago palm, 107
Saintpaulia ionantha, 16, 21,
  22, 28
Sand, uses of, 9, 18, 19
Sansevieria trifasciata, 21, 109
Saxifraga stolonifera, 22, 112
Scales, 5, 23. *See also* Insects
Scented houseplants, 24
Schefflera, 11, 22, 107, 119
Schlumbergera bridgesii, 11, 14,
  23, 45
Screw pine, 22, 108
Sedum morganianum, 39
Seeds, 5, 18–19
Senecio mikanioides, 65
Senecio rowleyanus, 114
Shamrock, Irish, 90
Shrimp plant, 109
Shrub verbena, 16, 80
Silver-nerve, 89
Sinningia speciosa, 18, 19, 21, 47,
  66–67
Slender lady palm, 78, 79
Slipper flower, 99

Slipper orchid, 79
Snake plant, 21, 109
Snowball cactus, 85
Soil, 5, 8, 9, 18
Solanum pseudocapsicum, 74
Soleirolia soleirolii, 34
Song of India, 98
Sorrel, wood, 90
Southern maidenhair, 84
Southern yew, 99
Spanish-bayonet, 124
Spathe flower, 110
Spathes, defined, 31, 87, 110
Spathiphyllum species, 110
Sphagnum moss, 14, 18, 22
Spider ivy, 22, 111
Spider mites, red, 5, 14, 23
Spider plant, 22, 111
Spineless yucca, 124
Split-leaf philodendron, 116
Spotted evergreen, 8, 44
Staghorn fern, 111
Staking houseplants, 16, 22
Standards, defined, 16
Stapelia species, 112
Star cactus, 68
Starfish flower, 112
Starfish plant, 112
Star flower, 73
Stem cuttings, 20, 21
Stem rot, 23. *See also* Root rot
Stephanotis floribunda, 83
Sterilizing, 8, 9
Stoneface, 82
Strap flower, 31
Strawberry begonia, 22, 112
Strawberry geranium, 112
Strelitzia reginae, 36–37
Streptocarpus species, 113
String-of-beads, 114
String-of-hearts, 105
Strobilanthes dyeranus, 95
Succulents and cacti
  aloe vera, 28
  aristocrat plant, 68
  beaucarnea recurvata, 102
  bird's-nest cactus, 85
  bottle palm, 102
  burn plant, 28
  burro's-tail, 39
  carrion flower, 112
  ceropegia woodii, 105
  Chinese rubber plant, 74, 102
  Christmas cactus, 11, 14, 23, 45
  Christmas kalanchoe, 11, 18,
    76–77
  crassula argentea, 74, 102
  crown-of-thorns, 51
  cushion aloe, 68
  devil's-backbone, 53
  Easter cactus, 45
  echeveria species, 56
  elephant bush, 102
  elephant-foot tree, 102
  euphorbia pulcherrima, 11,
    100–101
  euphorbia splendens, 51

Succulents and cacti *(continued)*
  euphorbia tirucalli, 85
  first-aid plant, 28
  flowering-stones, 82
  golden-star cactus, 85
  hairy toad plant, 112
  haworthia species, 68
  hearts-entangled, 105
  hearts-on-a-string, 105
  heart vine, 105
  humidity, 14
  jade plant, 74, 102
  kalanchoe blossfeldiana, 11, 18,
    76–77
  light, 11
  lithops species, 82
  living-stones, 82
  mammillaria species, 85
  medicinal aloe, 28
  milkbush, 85
  mimicry plant, 82
  mother-in-law's-tongue, 21, 109
  old-lady cactus, 85
  pearl plant, 68
  pedilanthus tithymaloides, 53
  pencil tree, 85
  pincushion cactus, 85
  poinsettia, 11, 100–101
  ponytail, 102
  portulacaria afra, 102
  propagating, 18, 22
  rainbow bush, 102
  rosary vine, 105
  sansevieria trifasciata, 21, 109
  schlumbergera bridgesii, 11,
    14, 23, 45
  sedum morganianum, 39
  senecio rowleyanus, 114
  snake plant, 21, 109
  snowball cactus, 85
  soil, 9
  stapelia species, 112
  star cactus, 68
  starfish flower, 112
  starfish plant, 112
  stoneface, 82
  string-of-beads, 114
  string-of-hearts, 105
  Thanksgiving cactus, 45
  toad plant, 112
  unguentine cactus, 28
  wart plant, 68
Suckers, 22
Summering houseplants, 15
Swedish ivy, 8, 114–115
Sweet potato, 8, 115
Swiss-cheese plant, 116
Syngonium podophyllum, 8, 31

T–Z

Table fern, 39
Tailflower, 31
Temperature, 13–14, 23
Ten-commandments, 103
Thanksgiving cactus, 45

Thousand-mothers, 22, 98
Threadleaf, 59
Tip cuttings, 19, 21
Ti plant, 116
Toad plant, 112
Tolmiea menziesii, 22, 98
Tradescantia species, 8, 121
Trailing watermelon begonia, 94
Tree ivy, 117
Tree-of-kings, 116
Trileaf wonder, 8, 31
Tuberous begonia, 19, 118
Tubers, defined, 19
Tuftroot, 8, 20, 21, 22, 54
Tulip, 118–119
Tulipa hybrids, 118–119
Umbrella palm, 119
Umbrella plant, 119
Umbrella sedge, 119
Umbrella tree, 11, 22, 107, 119
Unguentine cactus, 28
Unusual houseplants, 25
Urn plant, 27
Vacations, and houseplants, 15
Variegated laurel, 8, 11, 51
Velvet plant, 103
Venus's-flytrap, 120
Venus's-hair, 84
Verbena, shrub, 16, 80
Vermiculite, 9, 18, 19
Viruses, 23. *See also* Diseases
Vriesea species, 120
Waffle plant, 121
Wandering Jew, 8, 121
Wart plant, 68
Water and watering, 7, 8, 12–13,
  15, 18, 21, 22, 23
Water ivy, 65
Watermelon begonia, trailing, 94
Wax begonia, 122
Wax-flower, 83
Wax plant, 21, 122
Weeping fig, 17, 123
Whiteflies, 23. *See also* Insects
Widow's-tears, 19, 27
Winter-flowering begonia, 105
Wood sorrel, 90
Yam, 8, 115
Yellow sage, 16, 80
Youth-on-age, 22, 98
Yucca aloifolia, 124
Yucca elephantipes, 124
Zantedeschia species, 42, 110
Zebra plant, 124
Zebrina species, 8, 121

Have BETTER HOMES AND
GARDENS® magazine
delivered to your door. For
information, write to:
MR. ROBERT AUSTIN
P.O. BOX 4536
DES MOINES, IA 50336